PRAISE

It's with no small measure of praise that I say I stumbled across something great here. Steve Ferreira's latest book, *Navigating B2B*, is storytelling at its finest. Neatly packaged within the larger framework of a business-secrets manuscript, Ferreira's explosive storytelling will have you on the edge of your seat until the very end.
Julien Barbier | Co-Founder & CEO, Holberton

Navigating B2B is an electrifying journey through the whirlwind life of one of the most successful B2B navigators in the world. You'll learn a ton, you'll laugh even more, and at the end of the day you'll walk away shaking your head thinking, "No way! Did that really happen?!".
Glenn Hopper | CFO, Sandline Global

Well written book with very entertaining and poignant anecdotes, especially the stammering CEO which deeply resonated with me as I stammer as well.
Michael Dunlop | President & Founder, Net-Inspect LLC

Navigating B2B will be a fantastic addition to my library. If you're looking to get away from the cut and dry books on business success, you can't do much better than Steve Ferreira's crazy, global adventures.
Dennis Andrews | Founder & Partner, Scar Tissue

As thoughtful as it is adventurous, I was blown away by the compelling force of *Navigating B2B's* storytelling power. A definite must-have for any entrepreneurial library.
Lina Jasutiene | Managing Director and Founder, Recoupex

If there was one lesson I walked away with after reading Navigate! it was this: *never underestimate the power of the motivated, highly-creative individual.* It is the people crazy enough to play the game by their own rules, that eventually go on to shake up the whole system.
Kevin Hill | Executive Publisher, Freightwaves

Steve Ferreira approaches B2B relationships and all matters of entrepreneurialism with the poise, humor and good-natured attitude of someone who knows he's already won. A masterclass in confidence and execution, this was an extremely enjoyable read.
Christopher Weeklock | Executive Producer, Freightwaves

Steve Ferreira's latest work, *Navigating B2B*, gives us a glimpse into the kind of life we might lead if we were bold enough to take a gamble on the things we've quietly always wanted to accomplish. A masterclass in storytelling, Ferreira's humor and good-natured attitude are the glue that binds this impressive work.
Gordon Downes | CEO, NYSHEX

Unlike any other business book I've ever read! *Navigating B2B* has all the making of a best-seller with enough business insight to make it a must-have for executives the world over.

Bill Paul | Founder and Chairman, Logitalent

Good writing is hard to find. Good writing in a business book...well, let's just say it doesn't happen all that often. *Navigating B2B* was the exception. Not only was the prose splendidly put together, but the entire crazy, rollercoaster story also kept me on the edge of my seat from start to finish!

Tom Augenthaler | CEO and Founder, The Influencer Marketer

Steve Ferreira's book is captivating! The recounting of his life takes you quite literally all around the world and back, and you learn with him some of the most important, unorthodox and downright insane, life lessons for entrepreneurial success.

Michael Ford | Vice President, BDP International

Navigating B2B:

Master Your Industry, Your Business, and Yourself

STEVE FERREIRA

Copyright © 2021 Steve Ferreira
Published in the United States by Leaders Press.
www.leaderspress.com

All rights reserved. No part of this book may be reproduced or transmitted in any form or by any means, electronic or mechanical, including photocopying, recording, or by an information storage and retrieval system – except by a reviewer who may quote brief passages in a review to be printed in a magazine or newspaper – without permission in writing from the publisher.

ISBN 978-1-63735-041-6 (pbk)
ISBN 978-1-63735-040-9 (ebook)

Print Book Distributed by Simon & Schuster
1230 Avenue of the Americas
New York, NY 10020

Library of Congress Control Number: 2021900756

Dedication

For my wife Yulia and our children, Brook, Gabriel, and Sofia.

Contents

Introduction xi

1. Mind Mapping Childhood 1
2. Rhode Island's Finest Nighttime
   Establishment – The Foxy Lady 19
3. A Most Unorthodox Interview 35
4. What I Learned from the New York Mafia 51
5. The Stuttering CEO 67
6. Losing My Mind: The Seedy Underbelly of the
   Orient 83
7. From the Penthouse to the Basement 103
8. The Mental Jujitsu of Going Pro Bono 119
9. "No" Is Just A Yes That Needs More
   Convincing 137
10. "Oh Shit! We're on the Air?" 155

About the Author 173

Introduction

I've had an unusual life.

My path was not a straight and narrow entrepreneurial journey, but rather a series of labyrinthine twists and turns that have taken me all over the world and back. Throughout this incredible journey, I've had my fill of ups and downs, belly laughs and heartaches, and everything in between. Overall, I can say that it's been a life well-lived. However, when I sat down to write this book I was unsure of where I should take you, where to begin, and how to explain everything in a concise little business book. I looked at the big, trapezoidal shape that is my life story and just couldn't make heads or tails of how I would fit it inside the nice neat box of a "How to Grow Your Business" format.

So I didn't. I tossed that idea right out the window.

The stories you are about to read are not your everyday run-of-the-mill business lessons. There is no Bob and Sally by a watercooler in a skyrise office talking politics or company metrics. I don't know too much about that. It was never a part of my own story. Instead, I set out to tell the truth - the good, the bad, and the ugly. Over the course of my career as a solopreneur, I've been privileged to earn a fortune, silly enough to blow it all like a madman, and then wise enough to work like hell and get it back for my family. My journey has taken me from the continental United States to the far reaches of Eastern Europe and Asia, and just about everywhere in between. This book contains some of the biggest life lessons that I've learned along the way, particularly as they relate to professional business-to-business (B2B) relationships.

My hope is that you will see that the archetype of the entrepreneur is far broader and more widely inclusive than what we are typically shown. The people that are crazy enough to wear the title of entrepreneur do not fit inside a single definition – we are, by nature, trailblazers, rule breakers, creative thinkers, and unorthodox heretics of the business world. As such, not everyone founds their first company at twelve years old or learns how to build mainframe computers in their basement as a hobby. Some of us don't stumble upon our ideas until later in life. Some of us have to go out there and get the experience, cash our ticket, and ride the ride. Some of us had to live the story *first*, before we could come back and tell about it.

At the end of the day, this book is about communication, tapping into your strengths, challenging the status quo, going against the grain, and exploiting every possible ounce of your creative energy to make the life you've envisioned a reality. To aid in the learning process, you'll find a section at the end of each chapter titled **Putting It Into Practice**. Here, I review what I believe to be the biggest takeaways from my unique experiences in the business world. I encourage you to keep an open mind; find what works for you, and discard the techniques that don't. I can only explain what has worked for me, and in that same vein, I can tell the story in the only way I know how…

Welcome to my journey.

1 Mind Mapping Childhood

"I bet you have beautiful eyes," I said, in my best impression of a seductive purr. There was a sharp inhale on the other end of the line. I could hear the buzzing of innumerable telephones in the background, the crackling, popcorn-like sounds of dial tones and receivers picked up and put down. The female operator was trying admirably to do her job, to find out and direct the purpose of my call.

"Thank you. Now, how can I–"

"Tell me something about you, do you have kids?"

A momentary pause. I could picture the wheels turning in her brain.

Strictly speaking, operators weren't allowed to have personal conversations on duty, but everyone loves to talk about their kids, I reasoned. She cleared her throat a moment. "Well, yes, actually I do. I have…." Hook, line, and sinker.

It was 1974; I was fourteen years old.

Leadership Development: Operators and Alcohol

When I look back on my childhood, there seems to be a peculiar white void before and after the years surrounding my thirteenth through sixteenth birthdays. It's as if everything that came before and after was shot in black and white, and those three years were pure, saturated technicolor. Not to say I enjoyed them immensely; I didn't. But they stick out in my memory as being particularly formative, the beginning of a transformation or change that was starting to take place in me.

My childhood home was a cramped little thing in the spectacularly unassuming town of Taunton, Massachusetts, about forty miles south of Boston. There were five of us – my parents, my grandparents, and me - sharing a three bedroom, one bathroom floorplan. My father worked like a madman, splitting his time between three jobs, and my mother, busy with her own responsibilities, was also more or less absent. Usually, I found myself in the exclusive company of my crotchety old grandparents, or altogether alone. It was certainly lonely, but more than the lack of company, I remember the stupefying boredom.

The only real privacy I could find in that shamble of wood and shingles was the dark, dimly lit basement. Sporting small, rectangular slits near the ceiling for windows, it had a pronounced smell of mildew, which wasn't without a certain charm. Among its dubious trophies were my father's various medals from Korea, my grandfather's whipping belt (exactly what it sounds like), a fish tank, and a telephone. Let me tell you, loneliness and boredom can be one hell of a heady cocktail. It's amazing the things you can come up with to pass the time.

In my case, the game was telephonic journalism, or "The Art of Seducing an Operator."

In a very real way, the phone was my only link to the outside world. I was almost never allowed to go out into the neighborhood to play or have friends over at my house. So, instead, I'd pick up the phone book and scan through the list of hotels and department stores, dialing them up by region. "Hi, this is Steve Ferreira," I'd say, in my most official adult voice, "I'm an independent journalist and I'm conducting a survey of your working conditions. I was wondering if I could take a few minutes of your time…" The game was as much about keeping them on the phone, as it was about getting them to reveal personal details about themselves. Of course, at the end of every month I'd catch hell for the massive phone bill, but it was always worth it.

Eventually, it got to the point where I was on the phone so often I even developed a *regional preference* for these operators. For example, I learned that the ones in the Midwest were incalculably friendlier and much more willing to sit on the phone and chat with a polite stranger than the fiery women of the East Coast, who were about as amiable as a stepped-on snake. (*This would come in handy later on when I started my business, as I immediately sought out customers from the Midwest who were on the whole, more likeable and easier to talk to.*) My favorites, however, were the women in New Orleans who entranced me with their beautiful accents – I could listen to them yell at me all day. Standoffish as they were, it was always worth the call just to hear them talk for a while.

At the time, I didn't put much stock into my silly games. I was just bored and wanted someone to talk to. But gradually, little by little, I started to gain this immense confidence. I was discovering the power of my own voice. With that little kidney-shaped receiver in hand, I felt like I could reach anyone in the world; I was the velvet-voiced star of your favorite morning talk show, or the buttery voice of Sean Connery in *James Bond*. I had discovered the gift of gab, and as the saying goes, I soon realized I could sell feathers to birds.

As my confidence continued to grow, so did my boldness.

Bored as I was, cooped up in that house, I began an exhaustive search for even a modicum of excitement. I've always had a talent for finding and exploiting patterns: in numbers, languages, or human behavior. This is, to a large extent, what I credit for my success in business. But before that talent was translated to the likes of ocean freight shipping and invoicing, I first tried it out on my parents.

Perpetual creatures of habit, my parents visited Tony Parker's Supper Club every Saturday night. They'd eat, drink, and dance away the workweek in a greasy little speakeasy from 9:00 p.m. to 2:00 a.m. After months of veiled reconnaissance, I worked up the courage to try sneaking out. Given that it was my grandma and grandpa, both in their 80s, taking care of me (allegedly), it wasn't exactly like sneaking past the Gestapo. Drunk on teen bravado, I said to myself, "Hey, I'm gonna sneak out, walk to the end of the street, order myself a cab and I'll try and get some alcohol from a bar." It was a thing of beauty, really, the way it all worked out.

By ten o'clock, I'd be in the back seat of a yellow cab, cruising along to the bar. I'd spend my time tentatively sipping Jack Daniels and Coke for an hour or so, chatting easily with ladies of the night and bartenders. I looked much older than fourteen and easily passed for eighteen, the legal drinking age at the time.

Little did I know, this type of measured risk-taking was exactly the attitude I would bring to my future career. Between the telephone calls and the nightly "prison breaks," I was learning the value of coming up with a good plan, and more importantly, how to execute it flawlessly. I'll admit it was an unorthodox way to develop leadership qualities, but I've never lost sight of the value of those memories. During that period of my life, I discovered the power of my own voice: in an esoteric sense, but also very practically.

Speaking to full grown adults in a bar at fourteen years old, it was confidence or potential jail.

Experience has taught me that one of the main reasons people fail in business is they fail to plan three or four steps ahead. You've got to map out the objective, formulate what possible setbacks you might encounter, come in with your big guns, two or three things that are going to rock the world, and a few little provocative grenades to help restyle or reset the conversation if it gets off track. Most importantly, you have to recognize the checkered flag and know when it's time to jump ship and cut your losses.

My Father, the Three-headed Protagonist

Frank Ferreira was a short, bullish man with curly black hair who enjoyed his Winston cigarettes and silence. What he lacked in emotional communication (he seemed perpetually out of stock in the "I love you" department), he made up for it with his incredible work ethic and vigor. From as far back as I can remember, he split his time between being a janitor, a curtain salesman, and a bartender. As if that didn't keep him busy enough, he would often volunteer to do unpaid work. To him, it was a point of personal pride to make sure something was done right, financials be damned.

In July 1974, my dad was technically off work from at least one of his jobs. He had another month before his janitorial duties resumed at the nearby school. He seemed unable to sit still, pacing around the house like a caged animal. Eventually, he called the school principal and got authorization to purchase one hundred cans of paint. Over the course of the next month, he hand painted the entire school – for free. It wasn't his responsibility, but he wanted things to look nice. That's just how my dad was. Since I was practically a creature hiding in the basement at that point, I often got roped into these enterprises as well.

I ended up painting that school right along with him.

My favorite experiences were watching him in action as a salesman. He was really something when he got going, and I've often wondered what he could have accomplished with a little more education under his belt.

On the weekends my father worked for a Pakistani man that had made his fortune in curtains. He owned a factory in South Carolina where they were sewn and later trucked up the coast to Massachusetts. They had a cordial relationship, he and my father, primarily because the latter was so good at his job. He used to drive the women at the store mad, though not in the way you might think.

My father was the last person you might expect to show a natural talent for interior design. He was a gruff Navy veteran that smelled of sulfur and matches, but I'd be lying if I said he didn't know his way around a color scheme. Since the store's customer demographic was primarily women, he leveraged this visual prowess to identify exactly the right matching sets and complementary patterns to go with their pre-existing furniture. Looking back, I suspect they were both delighted and surprised to see a man like my father so eloquently versed in fabrics and color theory. What really made an impression on them, however, was his authenticity.

I remember one specific instance where this whirlwind of a woman burst into the store and demanded to, "See Frank, I have to see Frank Ferreira!" And because somebody else wanted to help her, she made a big stink about it: "I'm ready to make a big purchase, but I only want to work with Frank!" And so here I am, you know, amused by this woman's excessive theatricality: her bleached blonde hair, perfumed clothes, and expensive handbags. Clearly she had, shall we say, financial acumen. She probably could have bought the store herself if she'd been so inclined – it was a fairly cheap place. So, my dad came out and started to help her, asking about the details of the order she wanted to place. At one point, the woman had decided on a particular design, a rather expensive set for about $100. Quietly, almost under his breath, my father whispered to her, "You know, this $35 one is much better, and it's just about the same quality."

Even though he was paid on commission, he undersold her.

To put this in context, I have vivid memories of my scummy Uncle F. who would unashamedly try and convince his own sister-in-law (my mother) that I needed not the $15 pair of shoes for school, but the ones on the rack for $110. He was also getting paid on commission, the dirtbag.

In short, my dad had unshakeable integrity, and it paid off. That woman, with the fancy handbags and bleached blonde hair, came back again and again. Each time, she refused to see anyone but my father. It was a profound thing for me to witness at that age, as I realized that the selling process was about much, much more than just the product. People were sold on the person doing the selling as much as they were on the merchandise, and personality mattered a great deal.

Unfortunately for my dad, some of the places he worked were… shall we say, less than reputable.

The Knotty Pine, where my father tended bar on the weekends, was a lurid little establishment owned by my aunt and uncle. It reminded me of some sort of Satanic headquarters with its black exterior and eerie, white-shuttered windows. I never took a liking to the place and the inside did little to offset the overall effect. The downstairs had a green-tiled floor consisting of a bar, a small kitchen with a pizza oven, a grill, and a pool table. Upstairs, there was a bedroom with one bed, hundreds of *Playboy* magazines, and a pervasively odorous smell. It was an unspoken mystery who slept in that bed, given that the sheets were always rumpled and both my father and uncle were married.

If the Knotty Pine had any claim to fame aside from its impressively dilapidated appearance, it would have been my grandmother's Portuguese sausage – her *griesa*, as it's called. The hard labor in the bar came from her, and I vividly remember her cold fingers working over the greasy meat or shucking the clams in that cramped little kitchenette. It was the type of place you didn't want to spend too long in or you might just wake up fifty years older. It attracted the rough 2:00 a.m. sort of crowd – the cowboys, the bikers, and the factory workers. Usually, this wasn't a problem. My dad was the sort of no-nonsense, hardworking blue-collar man that other tough guys respected. Most of the time.

One day, my dad came home early in the morning from his bar shift with a pulsating lump on his head. After closing the bar for the night, someone had snuck up behind him and hit him square in the head with a tire iron; we never found out why. Though ugly to look at, my mother didn't think too much of it since my dad hardly ever complained. What we couldn't know at the time was that the injury had caused severe hemorrhaging in his brain. We ended up rushing him to the hospital where he received an emergency relief operation. He was never the same after that. The surgery left a jagged pink scar that remained despite his best efforts to conceal it. I hated that scar. I hated my uncle and aunt and their crummy bar. Most of all, though, I hated that my dad got hurt like that. It was a neon flashing reminder of why my dad needed to work three jobs in the first place, and why he had to put up with the dangerous and unseemly people that frequented places like the Knotty Pine.

I vowed to myself, then and there, that my life would be different. I respected my father, but I wouldn't end up in my fifties at a dead-end bar waiting for someone to crack open my skull.

No matter the cost, or how long it took me, I would do better than that.

Reinventing Your Own Wireframe

I asked for help, and God sent me Providence College.

Like many people before me, my experience of undergraduate education was precisely the kick in the ass I needed to get my life on track. Somewhere in the back of my mind had come the daunting realization that I had four years to get it all together, or I'd risk ending up back in the obscure anonymity of my middle and high school years all over again. Eight semesters, that was it. It wasn't so much that I set out to destroy my old self as much as I realized that if I was going to get out of this slump, if I was going to move beyond the limitations and hardships of my father's economic station, I would have to literally rewire my brain and my daily activities.

Luckily, I had an excellent college advisor named John. John was the kind of guy who was in exactly the right job for his personality; he had a wonderful knack for inspiring others and helping them find their way through, and eventually out of, the academic labyrinth. Like me, John was a visual learner, and so it was during one of our numerous talks about my career prospects that he introduced to me the idea of decision trees and flowcharts – sexy stuff, I know. What seems trivial or mundane, in retrospect, was in fact a great catalyst of things to come. Those flowcharts became my scripture; they were the maps that would show me how to move through the obstacles and impediments of my life (and they still are to this day).

I'd be the first to admit that I was never overly fond of being told what to do, or following what seemed to be unfounded, arbitrary rules. Writing and making charts were great ways to filter out the noise of adults and other busybodies who felt it was their mission to tell me where to step and in what size shoes. Starting from something as simple as a stick figure of myself, I was never much of an artist, I would make goal-oriented flowcharts complete with dates and small milestones along the way that would help me track my overall progress. The real beauty of the system, however, was not just that it presented me with an objective visual reference of my efforts, it taught me to anticipate disruption and plan for it accordingly.

For the first time in my life, everything seemed to be falling into place.

If John was the first person to open the door to my success, it was my college dormmate that eventually shoved me over the threshold. A native of Massachusetts himself, Rob grew up about twenty miles from my family's house. Despite the proximity, we'd never crossed paths before I arrived at Providence College. From day one, though, we took to each other like snow on a mountain. Rob was a smooth operator in all the ways I was not: he had excellent grades, had been the student council chairman for his high school, elected prom king, etc. He was one of those natural leaders that others instinctively gravitate towards. Unlike me, Rob already had a pretty good persona going into college.

Though we differed in some regards, Rob and I were just as crazy about charts and visuals – it was how we both processed decisions. For example, after Rob got an offer from Procter & Gamble to come work for their company, he ordered a case of their soap before giving them a reply, explaining to me that he "wanted to live the product" first. Unique as they were, his methods were fine by me. When US Lines offered me a job later down the road, we spent a week building a model ship from one of their cargo fleets, as we simultaneously examined the pros and cons of the offer. Two birds of a very strange flock, indeed.

Fortunately, Rob's natural confidence helped give me the courage to galvanize my own in many ways. Slowly, but surely, my youthful fearlessness in speaking to myriad phone operators began to return.

During summer break of our freshman year, I landed an internship at R.J. Reynolds Tobacco Company. Though I absolutely loathed cigarettes, courtesy of my father's habit, it was one of the best jobs I ever had. By the end of the summer, I had hatched the perfect plan to turn the internship into a full-time gig.

Pouring over the list of names in the local phonebook one Saturday evening, I found the name and phone number of the president of R.J. Reynolds himself, Paul Sticht. In a bold move that was to set the tone for everything to come, I decided I'd give him a call.

His wife answered on the third or fourth ring, and I asked if I could speak to Paul, as if we were old friends. In a good natured way, he got on the phone and listened while I introduced myself and prattled on about how much I had enjoyed working for his company during summer, and how much I had learned from the experience, blah, blah, blah. Impressed by my sheer audacity, he offered me a full-time position. The very next day, my immediate supervisor called me into his office and asked why in the world I would call the president of the company at home? He was trying not to be, the smile pulling at the corners of his mouth gave him away, but he was at least a little impressed. I told him the truth. "Jim, that's just me."

I learned by osmosis that if you really wanted to, you could reach just about anybody for just about anything. In that peculiar way, I had reached my own glass ceiling and smashed right on through.

My job at R.J. Reynolds reaffirmed the power of my own voice and instilled in me the necessity of selling in the way that was most authentic to me as a person. Eventually, I got so good at selling cigarettes that the owners would have me carrying around thousands and thousands of them in my car. I drove all around the state, paying visits to local business owners. They instructed, "When you go to a business that has a vending machine, we want you to take all the competitors' cigarettes out of it, and we want you to load our cigarettes in it." In order to do that, I had to get permission from the owners to convert the cigarettes from, say, Marlboro to Winston (R.J. Reynolds' brand).

That kind of selling was great for me because it encouraged my natural creativity. I was free to come up with whatever skit I liked, so long as the people kept buying from me. One way I often approached business owners was to bring my tools and clean their machines for free. After I'd finished, I'd say to them, "See, now your machine is crystal clear. It's so clean, I bet your customers can almost smell the flavor through the glass…it's just too bad you don't have something nicer to offer them." It was a line for sure, but the owners appreciated the spunk and the initiative and, more often than not, they'd let me fill their machines with R.J.'s products.

The crazy kid who cold-called the company president eventually became their number one guy.

Putting It Into Practice

My childhood taught me a lot of valuable lessons that I wouldn't really understand until much later down the road. It was an interesting part of my life, full of chaos, confusion, and a lot of trial and error. When I think back, it reminds me of a slow motion camera frame my parents bought me sometime in the early 1970s. It wasn't anything fancy – sort of a poor man's YouTube – but the short video was of a quarterback throwing a pass. What I liked about it was how you were able to manipulate the time by half second increments, forward or backward. By breaking down each sequence of motion, the camera was supposed to teach you how to throw the ball like a professional athlete.

Experience has taught me that our minds are just like that camera; we can train ourselves to quarterback each experience and record it, what went right and what went wrong. Even now, some fifty years later, after a bad phone call that doesn't go my way, I still think about that camera. I dissect the conversation into half second increments until I understand where I lost the other person, where I stopped perceiving their signals. Being an entrepreneur is a continuous series of evolutions; you grow, plateau, reevaluate, and then mush on. With each new iteration of your skill sets, the aim is to identify and refine those areas in which you already have proven value.

I still make mistakes, no doubt about it. But I could have never gotten to where I am today if I hadn't taken a brutally honest look at my own mind. I mapped it out, and here is what I found to be true thus far:

1. **Honesty and authenticity will get you further than any abstract sales technique or golden certification.** People can smell bullshit from a mile away; it doesn't do you any good to be anyone but yourself. As I learned from watching my dad sell curtains, people will respect you far more for your honesty and integrity than any far-fetched sales pitch or promise of riches to come. Find the thing that endears you to other people, and develop the hell out of it. Make *that* your "thing". Building a personal brand starts with identifying what sets you apart from other people. What unique value do you have to offer?

2. **Silence is a virtue.** If you're the one doing all the talking, be it in a business meeting, a date, a conversation with your kids, or anywhere else… something is wrong. Learn to listen. Punctuate your conversations with that most profound of silences: true listening. Not the kind of listening where you're gnawing at the end of a pencil stub waiting to get a rebuttal in, but rather the kind of listening that takes place when you are committed to understanding someone else's point of view. That's where the magic happens, where the formations of professional relationships manifest themselves.

3. **You only have to be courageous for one moment – the rest is endurance.** Make that phone call,

introduce yourself to that new partner, ask for help from those that know more than you. If it's something that scares you, chances are you're probably headed in the right direction. All it takes is one moment to get the ball rolling, after that, the inertia of that first step will carry you through. Trust your own instincts, you know more than you think you do. The power to act when you are afraid, to mobilize yourself in the face of anxiety, can be the differentiating factor between success and failure. How do you show up in the face of fear? What kind of strategies do you have for galvanizing your courage to take the necessary risks? Forget what you've heard, bravery is a quality that can be learned, developed, and perfected

4. **Telling a good story is worth its weight in gold.** It really doesn't matter your profession. Regardless of the industry in which you work, every single one of us has to sell something. Be it a product, a service, an idea, a brand, you name it. Everyone sells. And the thing about selling is, it all comes down to crafting a meaningful narrative. It's about grabbing someone's attention and giving them a reason to put their trust in you. The stronger your story, the more captivating your narrative, the more likely you are to succeed in your endeavors. My childhood taught me that when you are able to consistently weave a compelling narrative, particularly about yourself and your brand, people will follow their natural intrigue to be closer to you. And that means selling without trying to sell.

2 Rhode Island's Finest Nighttime Establishment – The Foxy Lady

The beautiful thing about college is the way it parallels, as its own separate little microcosm, the rest of the world at large. You can be ambitious, fall in love, have your heart broken, plan your future, start your career, and rage against "the man" all in the span of four years. In that way, it's almost a litmus test for the rest of life, an experimental backdrop where you get to play at becoming who you are. It's also probably the last time you can really screw around in a major way and get away with it.

And I took full advantage of that.

At nineteen or twenty years old and freshly liberated from the shackles of parental control, I was determined to find out what I could make of myself, what kind of person I could turn myself into if I really set my mind to it. There were the professional goals, of course – graduating, choosing a career, finding a good job, etc. What I didn't anticipate, though, were all the ways that college would bring out my propensity for theatrics, sometimes in more productive ways than others.

Not too far from the piously catholic campus of Providence College, flashed the lusty, pink neon lights of *The Foxy Lady* – the premier "Gentleman's Club" of the area. Once inside, its fully stocked bar, three stages, and combined 10,000 square feet came together to offer the feeling of stepping out of reality and into the slightly oily fantasy of a nightclub in East Berlin. I can't say with certainty the first time we stepped over the threshold into that ocean of sinful stimuli, but there was a feeling that this was *the place*. It wasn't so much the opportunity to rub shoulders with the "celebrity talent" there, it was the feeling of subverting some arbitrary and outdated rule. Each visit left us temporarily branded with an extra skin of glitter and a dark cloud of bad perfume that would stay embedded in our clothes for days. Needless to say, it was the best and the worst of places, the type of establishment where one might mosey up to an empty bar stool and sip the worst bottom shelf cheap vodka until your teeth fell out or your wallet was emptied.

Of course, neither Rob nor I had the cash reserves necessary to afford frequent trips to such an establishment. We were, by all accounts, dead broke – and so were all of our friends. Still, where there's a will, there's a way. I'm always amazed at the type of creative solutions you can come up with when you're strapped for resources. In our case, we were determined not to be swayed by something as trivial as money. We schemed and cajoled and planned. There had to be some way that we could get free booze, or a sort of discount membership, anything to offset the cost. After several weeks of our combined mental effort, we finally hit upon the perfect idea: we'd become the *male* dance act. Well, sort of.

Unfortunately, divine powers did not see fit to endow me with skills on the dance floor. As for Rob, well, you can imagine the awkward rigidity of two white boys practicing their imitations of pole dancing on each other. Nonetheless, the logic seemed airtight; since we couldn't afford to get in and pay for the drinks, we'd just find a way to work there instead. Who says college doesn't teach creative problem solving?

I never envisioned myself as an exotic dancer, and Rob and I furiously practiced our "routine" in the dorm room for hours. It was a harebrained idea from the start, fortified with copious amounts of beer and McDonalds. Since neither of us had any real experience in the world of provocative dance, we took our cues from the only source we knew: John Travolta in *Saturday Night Fever*. If you will, imagine two twenty-year-old boys bursting with cheeseburgers, french fries, and beer, gyrating their non-compliant hips to the Bee Gees' high pitched falsettos. Yes, it was a glorious thing, indeed.

Finally, the moment of truth arrived. We approached the manager of The Foxy Lady one evening and gave him our proposition. You might even say it was my first attempt at a sales pitch. The manager of the club was a short little man with a mustache like an ugly caterpillar on his top lip. He seemed none too amused with our antics as his bushy eyebrows pushed up towards the ceiling. He gave us the once over. After a long and thoroughly disconcerting look, we were given the green light to go ahead with our act (if you could call it that). We were brimming with false bravado and confidence, although I was hyper aware of the scantily clad women all around, watching as spectators. Before I knew it, Barry, Robin, and Maurice were coming in loud and clear over the speaker – it was show time.

We performed the whole thing fully clothed (both of us being too chicken shit to take anything off on stage in front of the girls). If we had been somewhat awkward and unrehearsed in our dorm room, the spotlight certainly did us no favors. I remember the prickling of sweat on my forehead as I tried to channel that exorbitant Travolta confidence. I was getting into the rhythm and my eyes squinted, the hazy lights carrying me on through. All in all, it was an absolute cringe fest. When the song ended, the adrenaline had us both shaking.

And then nothing.

No applause, no giggles. We were met with stupefied silence. The manager just stood there gawking at the two of us. I coughed into my hand a bit and told him, you know, we were just a bit nervous. We just got in from New York and, you know, it had been a long drive. There was a palpable tension in the air as he just continued eyeballing the two of us. He looked like a man about to make a very important decision. As luck would have it, we caught him in a good mood and though he pursed his lips at us for a bit longer, eventually he nodded his head and said real slowly, "You boys did good. Why don't you grab a seat… Enjoy the drinks and the girls."

He might as well have crowned us kings of Byzantium; we were on top of the world! For the rest of the evening we slugged back far too many drinks and kept a mental tally of all the money we weren't spending. It was one of the best nights of my life.

In retrospect, I don't believe he was impressed with our dancing. We never did anything more than that one audition. But, you could tell he respected the gall it took to pull off a stunt like that. Whatever his motivation, from that point on, admission and drinks were free. We were officially honorary members of the finest nighttime establishment on the Eastern Seaboard.

****

I bring this story up not to brag about my illustrious skills on the dance floor (you'd be hard pressed to find them, just ask my wife), but to illustrate what happens when you start believing in your own power. The Foxy Lady experience was fun, and certainly one of the more memorable highs from that time in my life, but I think the most significant takeaway was realizing that people seemed to respond well to my energy. I had been going against the grain all my life. I had been doing things that seemed odd or unusual to other people, but to me, it was like I had a hidden treasure map. I could see all the shortcuts. I understood how to approach a problem directly while also leveraging that part of me that thrived in a creative environment.

The Foxy Lady taught me that if you have the audacity to put yourself out there, to be vulnerable in a real, tangible way, people almost always react positively. People responded to my antics and my flair for theater because it was perceived as passion, and that, I knew, would get me somewhere.

The formula then, was fairly straightforward. If you just told the right story, at the right time, with a certain pizazz and confidence, people would usually buy it. In other words, I was free to be anything or anyone that I wanted, as long as I could convince other people of it. It was my first glimpse of narrative salesmanship as a life skill. After all, selling a product or a service was really just selling a story, wasn't it? And I'd been doing that since I was thirteen.

The Italian Chain Gang

As my short-lived dance career came to an abrupt end, I decided I would test this theory of passion and theater in more serious opportunities, ones that would help me prop up a future I was detailing on my flowcharts. Soon after, Rob - who was already a seasoned veteran of school politics from high school - became engrossed in his election campaign for Student Congress. The more I toyed with the idea, the more it began to make sense. I wasn't gifted with any particular athletic prowess, and it was pretty clear that there would be no athletic scholarship in my future. In terms of upward mobility, school politics was probably just as good as any other avenue. I even heard through the grapevine that several of the members of the Student Congress had gotten to meet President Jimmy Carter at the Oval Office.

That sealed the deal for me: forget dancing, I was going into politics.

Two years prior to my arrival, there had been a tragic fire on campus that cost the lives of several students. In a small private college like Providence, the loss was like an earthquake felt by the entire community. The incident had left an unhealed scar on the college's image and there seemed to be a general mood of despondency. Everyone, faculty and students alike, was on a soul searching quest to make sense of the lives that had been lost in the fire. I thought a great deal about what I wanted to say in my campaign and how I might tailor my message to be most effectively received. I thought a lot about that fire and about what it must have been like to be a student on campus when it happened. Once more, I returned to the power of crafting a meaningful narrative.

All at once, it came to me.

My campaign would be about personal growth and change. I knew what it was like to feel lost and uncertain. I had been picked on during most of my childhood, and when I wasn't, I was completely left to my own devices. I understood loneliness and the feeling of desperation and I used my experiences to tap into the collective unconscious of the school. By fusing their story of "redemption and revival" with my own, I gave vociferous speeches about how I would use this college experience as a means to reinvent myself. Like a phoenix, I would rise from the ashes of my old "trauma" and change the direction of the narrative. And, I explained, I wanted to take each and every one of them on that journey with me. The message struck a chord; I was reelected into office all four years of my undergrad. It seemed I had my finger on the pulse of the greater student body.

There's a lot more that goes into university student politics than I could have predicted. It took up an enormous amount of time and, at some points, negatively affected my studies. Still, for all that, it was an incredible experience. I learned how to lobby and how to sling my opinions into well-packaged slogans and bylines. I learned how to build a consensus from opposing viewpoints. As student treasurer, I learned the invaluable skill of investing and tracking money markets. Whether it was politics, sales, or an elevator pitch, life was steadily teaching me how to cultivate a personal brand image.

After a year or so of being involved in the daily happenings on campus, including the weekly congress meetings, there was one pressing issue that refused to give me peace: the quality of the food on campus sucked. I'm not trying to be melodramatic; it was just plain bad. When I approached other council members to see what changes we could enact, I was met with a practiced shoulder shrug and a forlorn look that said, "Well, what do you expect us to be able to do about it?" Once again, what appeared obvious to me was evidently invisible to my peers. Why go through all the chin-wagging and buttering up of university bureaucrats just to get a decent sandwich in the cafeteria, I reckoned to myself. Wouldn't it be more efficient and less-time consuming to just go directly to the head of the kitchen staff? If I had to bypass a few campus regulations in the process… well, it was for the greater good, wasn't it?

I can't speak to its current culinary representatives, but back then Providence's cafeteria was run by a motley, mean-looking crew of tight-laced Italians. They were the kind of guys that made you want to cross to the other side of the street if you saw them walking towards you late at night. The kind that wore black leather jackets and probably stuffed a silver stiletto knife into their socks. That is to say, they weren't the least bit intimidated by my scrawny twenty-year-old frame. What I lacked in physical stature, though, I made up in confidence. It was time to test out, once more, that golden gift of persuasion.

It started small. I would wake up at four in the morning and go with a friend of mine, a priest who was in charge of the male dormitories, to supervise the kitchen staff as they made the morning muffins. Over time they became more and more accustomed to my presence and I would make minute suggestions about what should be added or dropped from the cafeteria selection. "A little bit of applewood smoked bacon wouldn't hurt anybody, would it, guys?" I pressed. Inwardly, they were probably seething with rage. Who was this punk kid that was coming in and telling them how to do their jobs? In a way, they were right; I technically had no authority over their menu creation or inventory list. But that certainly didn't stop me from pointing out the inefficiencies of their procurement methods.

Speaking of methods, I had for some time harbored a sneaking suspicion that the head of the kitchen staff was getting some sort of lucrative kickback from a family member or friend for buying low-grade food in bulk. Why else would he continue buying what was obviously bottom of the barrel stock, week after week? I wouldn't have been against his little side hustle if it hadn't been directly proportional to the negative quality of the food.

One day, the conflict came to a head. The chef, if such an illustrious title could be granted to the man, demanded to know just who the hell I thought I was, telling him what to do? I was nothing more than a student, whereas he was a grown man and an employee of the college. Quick as a flash, I responded that I was on the food committee of the student congress. We had been, I continued, tasked with taking over the responsibilities of his procurement and ordering lists.

There was, in fact, no such committee.

The man seemed to sense this for a moment, and he wavered in his decision on whether or not to call my bluff. It was a tense moment, as he bit his bottom lip in contemplation. Finally, he let out his breath in a heaving sigh and a few Italian curse words followed. The deed was done. From that day forward, we ordered special cuts of meat, bacon by the cartload, and anything we thought the other students at the college might enjoy. At one point, we even convinced them to install a self-serve ice cream machine (which, back in 1980, was quite an awesome sight to behold). Yeah, we were manipulating the system, and certainly I broke a few rules in the process. When word finally got out to other members of the student congress, we were met with backslapping and congratulatory high fives. Unorthodox as the methods were, even the big wigs on campus recognized that all we were trying to do was drive positive change in the campus diet. The Italian street gang in the kitchen put up a small fight, a feeble resistance to protect their marginal profits. But with the entire college backing us, it was too late. I had looked for, and exploited, a noticeable hole in the system.

Game. Set. Match.

Putting It Into Practice

You might be thinking, "Ok, so you had some novel experiences in college, Steve. But what has this got to do with business?"

Everything.

Have you ever heard of the term peacocking? It refers to a type of social behavior where men dress in intentionally provocative or ostentatious ways to attract the attention of women. It's a crude, Neanderthal-like type of flirting for sure, but ask the dating experts…it's pretty hard *not* to remember the guy that showed up to the party in a leopard print suit. Where am I going with this? Be the leopard print guy! Be bold and willing to stand out in a targeted way. Often the greatest barrier between you and your potential B2B relationships is that first ice-breaking moment. It's getting past the logistics team and the virtual assistants and the ducked phone calls. We're living in an age where attention spans are getting shorter and shorter. People have less patience that they are willing to expend, particularly on strangers. They want bite-sized, ready-made meals and conversations.

My experiences in university and subsequent business ventures have reaffirmed my theories about the value of presenting yourself as an individual. From the long drawn-out phone calls with captive operators, to the theatricality of performing a strip tease for free alcohol, the underlying theme has always been the same: I was playing to the strengths and characteristics that make me unique. And you should, too. This has always been my gripe with books about sales. Unpopular opinion here, but they stink. They are robotic and way too rigid to be practiced in real life. If you want to make real, lasting connections with people, there is no substitute for authenticity and intrigue. Now, does that mean I parade into my business meetings with a flowing pink cape and an ascot? Absolutely not. However, here is what it does mean: I am willing to go above and beyond to get the attention of people I am interested in. I will think inside, outside and around the damn box if it means I can get my targeted message where it needs to go. In practice, this manifests itself in a variety of mediums, not the least of which is video and email content.

Several years ago I decided to invest about $10,000 into hiring an email expert that would bring my cold email campaign to the next level. The emails were designed specifically to bypass the choke point in my business – the corporate logistics teams – and get straight to the C-suite. I have an amazing computer guy in Poland who, for no petty sum, spends his days hunting email addresses for me off the potential customer list I always keep on hand. Between his expertise and the beautiful videography of my freelance professionals, I was able to carefully craft and curate personal elevator pitches to each company executive I was prospecting. In the video, I would succinctly and powerfully address glaring holes in their logistics and operations teams, drawing on the extensive research I'd done prior to contact them. In that way, I identified a problem of which the executive was unaware, and promptly provided a detailed solution as to how my business would remedy it for them.

I now have over fifty pages of tried and true attention-grabbing emails. I bring up these email campaigns to illustrate what I mean by circumventing the system. When I first started prospecting clients, if you wanted to reach someone outside of your network, cold calling was still very much the rage.

Thus, it was highly unusual to be creating customized video pitches via email. So unusual, in fact, that it worked like a charm. Those emails, which felt like a heavy investment upfront, have on average provided me with an additional $500,000 in revenue each year since their inception. And you know what? My quasi competitors hated it. In fact, they felt so strongly about my methods that they wrote an article on LinkedIn, acknowledging how effective the tactic was but complaining that it was "unethical" of me to sidestep the smaller players and aim right for the big shots. I was going against the SOPs, they said. It wasn't fair, they said. I'm sorry, but B2B does not wait for that bullshit. If there's a better, more efficient way to do something, I'm going to do it.

On that note…

Creative disruption has become something of a buzzword in our society today, but that does nothing to retract from its efficacy, in my opinion. The Jeff Bezos' and Steve Jobs' of the world did not color inside the lines, nor were they particularly concerned with standard operating procedures. When the rest of the world was going left, they went right. Each approached his business, his product, his service, and his company with his own personal brew of authenticity. The takeaway here is that no great entrepreneur has ever reached pinnacled heights by doing exactly what their predecessors have done before them. Make the system work for you. Challenge everything.

You don't have to be theatrical like me, or a computer genius like Jobs. What you bring to the table is your own unique set of talents, personality, and likeability – so lean in to them! Developing your brand is about being honest about what your strengths are and maximizing them to the fullest. You don't have to be the most talented, the most charismatic, or even the most intelligent. You just have to know what you're working with and how you can leverage those skills to solve pressing concerns for your persons of interest.

I challenge you to always question why things are done the way they are before you passively accept them as law. The system is made by humans, and we are an inherently flawed species. If you pay attention, stay focused, and always remain at the ready for the next professional opportunity, I promise your chance will come. And when it presents itself, don't be afraid to show a little audacity. The universe rewards undaunted acts of human courage.

3 A Most Unorthodox Interview

Entrepreneurs are a funny bunch of enterprising individuals. They are the round pegs that rarely fit into the square holes society loves to manufacture, ad nauseum. As a result, these rebellious types often end up becoming the catalyst of major creative disruptions in their industries. The irony, of course, is that we celebrate the very same individuals who seem to defy the rules and systems we are taught to abide by. Yet, it is exactly this kind of lawless bravado that we love to hear about in the corporate world. Just think about how saturated our culture is with underdog stories, eclectic geniuses, and overnight billionaires. We eat it up every time. There's something to be said about being unapologetically yourself that strikes a universal cord with people.

Recently, I stumbled upon an interesting example of this in an article from entrepreneur.com:

****

Craig Handley, CEO of Listen Trust, had a singular goal: he was going to meet Sir Richard Branson. If you're not familiar, Richard Branson is the founder of Virgin Records, a successful entrepreneur whose estimated total worth is in the hundreds of billions of dollars. Thus, it was not exactly an easy appointment to make. Undaunted by such a trivial barrier to entry, Handley executed a plan that was arguably a stroke of pure genius.

When Richard Branson came to speak at the Direct Marketing Association in San Francisco, you can bet your ass that Craig Handley was there as well - and not just as a spectator. Actually he was dressed to the nines in the outfit of a security guard. The plan was to sneak backstage and try to catch some face time with the business tycoon (talk about throwing caution to the wind!) After Branson had given his speech, Craig walked right up to him and handed him a business card with a $20 bill wrapped around it. Without missing a beat, he shook the hand of his idol and said, "This is the first $20 we're going to make together." Branson was a good sport about it; he laughed and pocketed the business card (and the $20 bill) before giving Craig his personal email address.

Fast forward a few years in time, and Craig's business is doing quite well. Seemingly out of the blue, he receives an invitation to Necker - Richard Branson's private island! That's right, not only did he remember the gesture, he thought highly enough about the guy to share his private island with a virtual stranger for a week. When Craig joked with him about pocketing that $20 bill, Branson just smiled and said, "I didn't become a billionaire by refusing money when it's offered to me."

Since then, Craig has visited Necker half a dozen times with a myriad of other successful entrepreneurs.

****

What I particularly love about this story, and why I included it here, is that I think it encapsulates everything that is innovative, bold, and unconventional about the entrepreneurial mindset. Like Handley, I have been predisposed to a few theatrical liberties in my own professional career, and more often than not, they have paid off tremendously. Actually, I consider this flare for the dramatic to be one of the most underutilized weapons in the vast array that is the entrepreneurial arsenal.

I first became privy to its power in a few, shall we say, unorthodox interviews that I had during my senior year at university. Let's take a stroll down memory lane for a moment….

John

I've mentioned him before, but I'd like to go back for a moment and talk about him in a bit more detail. John, if you'll remember, was the career outreach counselor at Providence College. Physically, he was the nerdy sort of character that had the unfortunate tendency of disappearing into the background, and his thirty years at the college hadn't helped that one bit. If anything, it turned him into something like the human equivalent of a barnacle on the side of a rusting ocean freighter (I say this with all respect, if there are stratified classes of barnaclehood, then John was of the very best kind). Beyond his physical appearance, John was a veritable Mr. Miyagi; he had the type of sagacious and unassuming wisdom that defines great men. That is to say, John had the perfect disposition for the type of career he had chosen.

Unfortunately, because of his quiet demeanor, most of the students flat out ignored him or never knew he existed in the first place. But there was something that drew me to the man from the very beginning. When it came to doling out career advice and tactical strategies for crushing job interviews, John was nothing short of brilliant. He was quite possibly my first real mentor. As a result, I stuck by him closely all four years of undergrad, hoping that I would absorb some of that wisdom through proximity or sheer osmosis.

About two years before my graduation, John persuaded me to take an interview with a friend of his in New York who was the president of a major textile company. By this time he had consistently and strategically hyped me up, bolstering my confidence with affirmations that I was definitely on track to have a fantastic career. "There's something positively unique about you," he would say. Whether it was true or not was of little consequence. He was the only person in my life at the time who was really willing to bet it all on me and for that, I was awash with gratitude.

Though I was only in my junior year, I agreed to take the interview with his friend. The next week I jumped on a bus and made the two and half hour commute to New York City. Over the course of that afternoon, I interviewed with five or six executives from various departments. I'd love to be able to tell you that I rocked it, that I went in there and mopped the floor with my competition. I did not, however. In actuality, I was a bonehead in those interviews and really said some stupid things. I was young and very much out of practice.

Unsurprisingly, they opted *not* to offer me the job.

I returned to Rhode Island with my tail between my legs, thinking that not only had I let my mentor down, but I'd completely biffed my first major interview. It felt like a kick in the teeth. My grandiose plans for the future had, for all intents and purposes, been dashed in one fell swoop. When I reluctantly dragged myself into his office to tell him all about it, John just laughed at me in a kind way. "Look at the bright side," he said. "Now you've talked all the stupidity right out of you! I bet you won't make that mistake next time, will you?" I couldn't help but laugh at that. He was right, I was being a bit melodramatic about the whole thing. More importantly though, he opened my eyes to the deeper lesson of that experience: never, ever, would I go into an interview unprepared again.

Making Waves

My parents were not ambitious people in the traditional sense of the word. My mother, who worked at a factory for as long as I can remember, was of the same blue-collar background as my dad. It was never clear to me whether they had once had dreams and fantasies of their own – if they did, they certainly didn't talk about them to me. One value they both shared, however, was the notion that I was going to receive a higher education. As an only child, my parents funneled every available penny that wasn't going toward bills, debts, or general subsistence, into a college fund that would hopefully one day elevate me beyond our current economic position. They might not have been overly affectionate, but I'll be damned if they weren't invested in my education.

Their investment had a profound effect on me. By the time I was ready to graduate, I felt as if there was an immense, invisible anchor around my neck: the weight of their expectations. My mind burned with a manic fever as I thought about the approaching graduation day. I absolutely, unequivocally, needed to find a job. And not just any job, either. I had to find one that would pay back (if not financially, then at least emotionally) all their years of hard work and sacrifice.

Providence College received a number of visits in the early 1980s from reputable Fortune 500 companies seeking to cherry pick fresh talent right off the graduate assembly line. Companies such as *Procter & Gamble*, and *Time* magazine offered a few of the more prestigious and well-known opportunities. Today, the professional landscape has changed significantly and the most sought-after jobs are for innovative technology companies like Google, Apple, and Amazon. Back then, however, getting offered even an entry-level position at *Time* was like having Elon Musk compliment you on your theoretical equations. It was a big deal.

To sign up for interview opportunities, all you had to do was put your name on a roster next to a corresponding date and time. Roughly two years had elapsed since my "mishap" at the textile company in New York. My splintered confidence had fully healed, and I was ready to take another stab at the art of professional interviewing.

Unfortunately, so was half of the student body.

The lines to get your name on the interview rosters extended well out into the campus greenery. When I ventured a glance at the names on the list, my stomach did that type of frightful roll where your insides seem to shift and squish around your diaphragm. "Fuck, I don't stand a chance," I thought bitterly to myself. The pedigree of student that had signed up was, on average, destined to solve world hunger, cure cancer, and become a Nobel Laureate before they even hit forty years old.

Most of these kids came from families where their mom or dad were already CEOs, senators, or held other illustrious positions. I, on the other hand, was a solid B student who came from the backwaters of a forgotten town in Massachusetts. My greatest strength, I reasoned, was the sharp tongue I had honed from the verbal warfare of student congress. I was a scrappy junkyard dog, but I wanted it so bad… I wanted to knock it out of the park for myself, for my family, for my dad and all those crummy jobs he had to work to put food on the table.

The starting salary for *Time* magazine was $16,000 (roughly the equivalent of 75k by today's standards). I didn't have a snowball's chance in hell, but I signed up anyway.

The days passed, and slowly but surely, the appointed hour was drawing near. The night before the interview, I remember sitting in the dorm room berating myself for putting my name on the interview list. In terms of preparation, I still had yet to so much as pick up a copy of *Time* magazine, let alone actually practice my responses. I was absolutely sure that when I opened my mouth, something stupid was going to come out. I had a pity party of one and didn't sleep very well that night. At five o'clock the next day, the day of the interview, I finally had my eureka moment. It was going to be unorthodox, it was going to be radical, it was going to be downright strange… but it might just work. I hustled down to the store and bought a few last minute items.

A Most Unorthodox Interview

The moment of truth arrived.

I'm sitting on an old, creaky wooden chair, dressed to a spotless shine in my suit and dress shoes. My palms are sweaty and I can't believe what I'm about to do. Just then, out walks Liz Flynn, our valedictorian, through the French doors. I can see the panel of interviewers behind her for a moment as the door clicks shut. She's positively beaming, her smile cresting ear to ear. "I nailed it!" she says triumphantly. We all nod our heads and pretend that we are as stoked for her success as she is. Next up is Peter. He goes in and a half hour later, he too comes out looking for all the world like they already offered him a job as Editor in Chief. I'm wound tight like a spring now. The pressure is on and it's too late to turn back.

Finally, my name is called and I stride confidently into the interview room, my head held high and my black leather briefcase in hand. The *Time* representative is a short, pudgy man with a strange mustache and a sports coat. He extends his hand to me, and mumbles a practiced "hello". I pay him no mind, refusing to even make eye contact. Instead, I lay my briefcase down on the smooth wooden finish of the desk, release both of its golden clasps, and pull out two magazines: *Time's* latest issue and that of their competitor, *Newsweek*. Only now do I look up at the recruiter. He's giving me the type of bewildered look that I expected.

Good. Everything is going according to plan. I'm in control.

While I have his attention, I slowly and ever so carefully lift the *Time* magazine from the table. With his eyes still glued to the glossy cover, I proceed to rip it into twenty little pieces before tossing it on the floor. The poor man is now completely flabbergasted by my exhibition. I give him no quarter, though. "Mr. Smith," I say, addressing him for the first time. "I'm about to show you how effective I would be working for your competitor, *Newsweek*." I spent the next twenty-five minutes selling him on all the advantages that *Newsweek* had over *Time* from a readership prospective. Point by minute point, I detail the things that I have noticed that *Time* does poorly and how I would fix it. To his credit, Mr. Smith took my passionate diatribe like a gentleman and didn't interrupt once, until we were approaching the end of my thirty minute allotment. Finally, he held up a hand to motion that he wanted to get a word in edgewise.

He looked at me, trying his best not to smile and said, "You mind if I asked the questions now?"

He spent the last four minutes going through the formalities of a normal interview, asking about my background, my interests, and my career aspirations, etc. It was all par for the course and we both knew it. Before I left that office, he offered me the job.

It was at precisely that moment that I learned what happens if you dare to strike out and be different.

After I got the offer from *Time*, I thought to myself, "Well, now I can do anything I want because I have a guaranteed offer." I found that by using all those props, I was giving off much stronger signals and the general reaction was that at the very least, this was a very interesting marketing approach. And so, when Procter & Gamble came to the campus, I did the same thing with them. Only this time instead of a magazine, I brought a tube of Crest toothpaste and a tube of their toothpaste, and I squirted theirs into the garbage can before explaining exactly why Crest was a better product. Procter & Gamble offered me the job as well.

I was on a roll!

The offers from *Time* and Procter & Gamble were for an equivalent $16,000 starting salary. They were both extremely tempting and either position would have made my family proud. Before the end of the week, however, another company had come to Providence's campus: United States Shipping Lines. U.S. Lines was an ocean freight shipping company (see where this is going?) and they were offering a whopping $32,000 starting salary! Once I heard that number, it was like bells started going off in my head. I would get that job, whatever it took. I pulled no punches. Forget a tube of toothpaste or a magazine, I said to myself – I built an entire freaking model ship instead. Not just any model ship, mind you, an exact replica of one of their ocean freighters. This I proceeded to smash into a million little pieces during the interview. Their reaction was, once again, exactly what I had been expecting. I followed this demonstrative display with a polished speech about how I would rebuild the company with my marketing ideas. It was bold, vicious, guerrilla-style interviewing. Two men, one desk, mano a mano.

U.S. Lines offered me the job, and I accepted on the spot. So began my career in the world of international freight shipping.

Putting It Into Practice

A few years ago I decided to start teaching my kids about improvisational thinking, a tool that has been invaluable in my own career. As I considered how best to approach the subject, I once again got to thinking about acting, theater, and improv. After all, aren't performers the very best people to study from if you want to learn how to think on your feet? The more I turned it over in my mind, the more it seemed to make sense. So, one evening at dinner I gave it a shot. I turned to my kids and said, "I'm going to go into the pantry closet over there and when I come out, I'm going to do a play for you guys." As you can imagine, they were quite thrilled at the prospect of watching dad play the fool. Their excitement was practically palpable in the air. "What should the play be about?" I asked them. "It should be about a robot that eats alligators!" my oldest boy yelled at the top of his lungs.

Whew! A tall order, indeed.

I slunk into the kitchen pantry and stuffed on rubber gloves and some goggles, choosing from a potpourri of cleaning and culinary appliances. I decked myself out as best I could in the likeness of the galaxy's most formidable alligator-eating robot. After a few minutes of preparation, I grumbled out of the closet and roared around the kitchen in my best monotone voice, pretending to munch on the spiked tails of vanquished gators. As one might have expected, the kids loved it.

What did it feel like, as a grown man, to play dress up? A bit awkward for sure. There was the tendency to get tense and self-critical, but as I got more and more comfortable, deciding to just be present in the moment, my body relaxed. I learned to think on the fly and just go with it. After what seemed like a few hours, but was actually ten minutes, I passed the torch to my kids. They each had to come up with their own play: no rehearsal, no planning, just on-the-spot improvisation. We've been doing this now for years.

I've long been a believer in the power of effective storytelling. It's one of those skills that transcends industry, race, gender, nationality… it's a common and universal truth of the human experience. Personally, I think there is no better avenue in which to learn communicative storytelling than from acting. Maybe the two don't necessarily jive in your mind, theater and sales, but they are one and the same. Anybody that wishes to get good at business, at least in my opinion, should seek out novel social experiences. By novel, I mean all those instances where you're going to be awkward, uncomfortable, perhaps out of your depth. That could be playing dress up with your little ones, or trying an open mic night at a comedy club, or even doing some public speaking at your company events. The method is not nearly as important as the frequency with which you practice.

Train yourself to remain calm under pressure, to put other people at ease, and watch how much more effective you can become with your communication.

A sales strategy/process with nineteen and three quarter steps? I don't buy it. A book with vectored images of the ideal sales approach? Miss me with that, too. The truth is, you can drop me in any interview in the world, any client-facing meeting with nothing but a piece of construction paper, some glue, and a marker or two, and I'm confident I will come out victorious. It's not because I am a gifted artist, or because I'm an egotist with a bloated head (mostly true). It's because I believe in the value of what I am selling – myself! I believe in my own work ethic, my ability to think on the fly, and most importantly, my ability to solve problems in real time.

When I think back to those interviews in college, I am very much reminded of Craig Handley and the way he tailored his approach to Richard Branson. It was bold, theatrical, and definitely charismatic. I'll tell you what else, though. I bet Craig was scared shitless when he was doing it! I know I was during those college interviews. It's not at all comfortable to stand out in such a pronounced way, to go against the grain and be so radically different from your peers. But that's where the magic happens. That's where creativity meets ingenuity and coalesces to form the type of leader that other people can't help but be drawn to.

I'm not advising you to go out there and start dismantling your company in full view of the CEO or your board of advisors – that's not really the lesson at all. Instead, what I'm saying is that it's all right to be the round peg that doesn't even try to fit into the square hole. Embrace what makes you different, turn it into a profitable weapon. We hear it so often now that it's almost become white noise, but every single one of us is unique. The way to become successful, then, is not to try and emulate the people that you love and respect. In reality, those people you admire were unwavering in their dedication to their own personal compass. Sure, they took advice from other people and had mentors, but at the end of the day, they remained true to their own personal flavor. That's what makes them successful. That's what you need to tap into.

If there is one thing I've learned over the years it's that whether you're trying to pick up a girl, drive a ball down the fairway, lead a company, or smash an interview…more often than not people will respect you for the audacity you showing in coloring outside the lines, provided you do it with confidence.

Be the round peg; there are plenty of squares out there getting along just fine. They don't need your help. What the world needs is what you alone can offer. That uniqueness, that flair, that dramatic oomph that leaves people thinking, "What the hell was that?" as they smile and shake their heads in disbelief.

That's what you have to offer.

4 What I Learned from the New York Mafia

"The other Dons in the room applauded and rose to shake hands with everybody in sight and to congratulate Don Corleone and Don Tattaglia on their new friendship. It was not perhaps the warmest friendship in the world, they would not send each other Christmas gift greetings, but they would not murder each other. That was friendship enough in this world, all that was needed."

Mario Puzo, *The Godfather*

****

Whether I was pushed, cajoled, or went into the box willingly, I cannot remember. I do know that I was inspecting the integrity of the container, looking for holes in the corrugated steel that might let water or other unwanted residue contaminate the cargo. Even with the metal doors opened to the breeze, the heat and humidity inside were staggering. I stood there in my suit and tie, head cocked towards the ceiling with a flashlight in hand. Before I had time to react, there was the eerie and deafening groan of old metal being forced to give way. The light fled from the container like blood from an opened artery. I whipped around just in time to watch the rusty latch of the iron lock snap into place. I could hear them snickering in the background, drunk and playing their games.

The absence of light was so complete that I couldn't see my hand in front of my face. My heart thumped against my ribs in a way that made me uncomfortably aware of its tempo. The sweat, which had been small rivulets at first, turned into persistent tributaries that gathered momentum as they were pulled down by gravity over the knotted muscles of my back. I swallowed hard. The heat seemed to constrict the tie at my throat. I gagged reflexively, choking on the stale, rusty air. The urge to panic was threatening to overtake me; my brain screamed furiously in protest for more air, less heat, a breeze, some light, anything!

It was the dead of summer, and the New York Mafia had just locked me inside a shipping container.

****

Welcome to the Big Apple

I don't care if you're a goat herder living in India, a fisherman prowling the Cuban shores, or a Parisian housewife munching delicately on your croissant – at some point in time, everyone has had a fantasy about living in New York City. I was certainly no exception. Growing up just outside the reaches of Boston, New York City was the ultimate horizon line of my childhood. Just a few short hours away from my tiny home in Taunton, New York seemed to pack the promise that there, and only there, you could find everything that was good and worth doing in the world.

So you can imagine that upon graduating and taking a job with U.S. Shipping Lines, I was overjoyed to be doing my training in NYC. Hell, it didn't even take a lumen off the shine that I would be working all my days on the wharf and not in the illustrious skyscrapers of Manhattan. As far as I was concerned, I got to wear a suit and tie to work, and I was living in the big bad city as a freshly minted college graduate. Life was decidedly hopeful.

If you've never had the pleasure to wake up early and smell the rotting stench of fish and professional seamen, I invite you to take your next leisurely holiday at the Port of New York. To the untrained eye, it can feel like an overwhelming cacophony of moving steel and corrugated tin. It's like watching the polar ice caps break up, these tectonic giants with their boisterous motors that churn the waters of the bay and the gasoline and diesel plumes that crest upwards towards the sky. The sheer size of the freights and the stacked cargo they carry, like brightly colored Legos, gives one the impression of standing at the feet of mythological creatures. It's no Sistine Chapel, but it is truly a marvel to behold in person.

I'd be remiss if I gave such a stirring account of the proprietary vessels of the harbor without commenting on the colorful and nefarious-looking longshoremen. This class of men seemed to belong to the violent prehistoric past; you don't get much tougher than the guys that work the docks in New York. The vast majority had bodies littered with enough scars to liken a resemblance to a topographical map. Their faces told the stories of bar fights, tire irons, and busted lips. That said, I've also never been around a group of more darkly humorous individuals in my life, and if I learned anything from them it's that there's something to be said about the palliative quality of gallows humor. In that respect, these guys were professional ball busters. As a twenty-two-year-old kid in a fresh pressed suit, sweating through every single layer of fabric on me during the blistering heat of summer… Well, you could say I was an easy target for their jokes.

In the Company of Made Men

At one point in my life, I had a girlfriend who was absolutely convinced that I was something like a lieutenant or an obscure invisible player in the criminal underworld. In a lot of ways, ocean freight shipping can be like that. There's the late night phone calls, the barely contained anger when some "precious cargo" has been "lost" somewhere in transit at sea. There is the extortion of invalid charges and expected port official bribes. In many ways the two parallel one another. Truth be told, however, I had never been even tangentially associated with the idea of the mafia or any other body of organized crime. My most profound experience in that regard was making it through the heartbreaking evolution of Michael Corleone's self-destruction in *The Godfather* (parts 1, 2, and 3).

But all that changed in 1983.

I showed up for work as usual one morning, wearing my crisp blue suit and brown oxford dress shoes. The waterfront was calm and still in the early hours of the dawn, not yet primed to its usual state of activity and hubbub. I began making the rounds of the vessels, inspecting the containers and the logbooks of various freights, when I noticed something unusual. There, on the docks of the waterfront, next to the bow of an enormous container ship, a gang of greasy looking tough guys were fishing off the pier. Fishing…in the New York Port. Well, you see something new every day, I supposed.

As I came down the gangplank, I caught the eyes of some of the would-be fishermen. I returned their stares with muted curiosity. Who the heck were these guys and what were they doing fishing on a commercial pier? Each was dressed in nearly the same style: plain t-shirts, dirty work boots, and a package of cigarettes rolled into their sleeves, James Dean style. "Aye, pretty boy, that's a nice suit yuz got there," one of them called with an accent thicker than peanut butter. The others all chuckled at the mild ribbing and waited to see how this young buck would react. "You kidding me?" I hollered back. "This monkey suit's choking me from the neck down, be a wonder if I can still have kids after I quit this job." That got them going real good, and we traded a few witticisms back and forth there on the dock.

That was my first encounter with anyone from the New York Mafia. But it wouldn't be my last.

I can't really tell you what it was about, maybe they just saw something in me, or maybe it was because I didn't act afraid of them. Where other people would shy away, I walked right up and shot the shit with those tough guys, asking them all kinds of questions which they generally didn't answer. Whatever the reason was, from the first day I met them, this group of made men took a liking to me and took me under their wing, so to speak.

Over time our relationship became positively chummy. I was still an executive in training, so I could never ditch the suit, but the mob guys didn't give me a hard time about it after that initial encounter. They saw I was breaking my back every day for the company, and I think at some level they respected my work ethic. That being said, they also took it upon themselves to "relieve me" of said hard work whenever the opportunity presented itself. "Hey, you know you don't have to work that hard, don't you?" they chided me often. "Come on kid, let us show you how the shipping business *really* works, the easier side of life." It didn't matter if I protested or not, once they made up their minds, I was going where they were going.

As if to make the whole thing official, and ya know, relieve some of my mental burden, they'd even go and get "permission" from my boss at U.S. Lines. In a pack of three or four, they'd crowd his office like a gang of wolves, smiling dangerously as they told him with bared teeth, "Hey pal, we're taking Steve out for a drink today, we'll bring him back later on." My poor supervisor just stood there helpless as a lamb. There was no way in hell he was about to tell these professional tough guys to get lost, that I had a job to do. I would think to myself, holy cow I can't go out drinking right now, it's ten in the morning. I even tried discreetly to tell my boss what was going on. "Hey, I just want you to know that I'm not associated with these guys in any way, you know, I don't even want to go out drinking with them. I can just go back to my shift and…" The poor man was so traumatized, he'd pull me aside and with a deadly serious look in his eye he'd tell me, "If those guys want you to go, then you go. You go. No questions asked."

So I went every time.

In theory, I knew these guys were probably not of the highest moral caliber. Though they kept their jokes and stories censored to a decidedly PG-13 level when I was around, there was enough intonation and nuance to know that beyond the easy smiles and endless litany of jokes, these were not people you wanted to mess around with. Still, for all that, I loved it. I felt like I was part of a small team or a family, which sort of made sense because the majority of them were bonafide family guys with wives and kids and the whole nine yards. Often, they'd take me out and play ball or teach me to fish – the type of stuff that my own dad had never done with me. They never really busted my balls or gave me a hard time, they just accepted me as a sort of pet or mascot. They never did ask me to join their gang, but for the entirety of my working life in New York, I was something of an honorary member in their comings and goings. Ironically enough, on the whole, I never felt safer. When I was with those guys, nobody could touch me.

Actually the only real danger was the mafia guys themselves.

I can't tell you how many times we went to the same crummy, back-alley dive bar. We'd sit around a large circular table and play cards and drink beer while they chain-smoked caches of cigarettes. They didn't clue me into their plans or talk about their scores or successes in the "industry". I didn't hear about killings or who was set to get whacked that week. We were there to gamble and have a good time. And for the most part, I toed the line fairly easily.

One night, when just me and one other guy were driving back to the docks, I mustered up the courage to ask a direct question. "So," I said casually, "tell me more about this mafia business, what's that like?" We were cruising down the highway at 70 mph. The car was positioned so that it was dead in the middle of five lanes of traffic. Yet, in the time it took the man next to me to throw daggers with his eyes, he had weaved recklessly through all five lanes until he came to a screeching halt on the right shoulder of the road. The entire maneuver had taken about two seconds flat. He didn't touch me – he didn't have to. The man just looked at me and said, "Don't you ever say that again." And that was the end of it. He started the car back up and we drove on into the night.

Whatever protective bubble I had been inhabiting seemed to pop right then and there. These guys were nice enough on the surface, but that conversation left me with the indelible impression that none of them would think twice about plunging a knife into my guts if it meant less trouble for their organization. I was shook up in a big way and tried my best not to let it show.

Hell is a Hot Metal Box

There is the deafening sound of rusted metal being forced to move against its will....I turn back just in time to see the last sliver of sunlight amputated from inside the steaming metal box.

The absence of light is complete; I can't see my hand in front of my face. In the darkness, I can feel my heart slamming against my rib cage, angry, terrified, possessed. My breath is coming in shallow, staggered spurts. As often as I reach up to wipe the sweat from my eyes, it is replenished anew with a fresh, salty stream. I am trying not to hyperventilate, trying not to lose my cool. I rip at the tie around my neck; it's starting to choke me. I slide off the suit jacket and unbutton my collar. My back is knotted and tight from stress. The heat inside the container is thick and oppressive. It must be well over one hundred and twenty degrees. Time slows down, everything slows down in the darkness. Ten minutes pass, then twenty, then thirty. There's only so much air in a closed shipping container; I should know, it's my job. I can hear the idiots outside, laughing and telling jokes. "They don't actually want to kill me," I say to reassure myself. It doesn't work. Whether they want to or not, all of them are drunk enough to forget that they've left me in here. I could suffocate in less than an hour. My brain is screaming furiously in protest. I need air!

WHOOSH!

Without warning or preamble the silence of the container is cracked like roaring thunder, as the metal doors are pried open. The air itself seems to heave and sigh as my face is blasted with a cool maritime breeze. I could quite literally cry from relief, but instinctively I know that the next moments are critical. They will decide my fate.

I gather up the last reserves of my courage as I swagger out of the metal container, soaked to the bone and dripping with sweat. There's a gang of mafia guys all gathered around, their eyes trained on me. "How's he going to react?" their looks seem to say. Is he "with it" or is he going to get angry and lose his cool. All of this is taken in in a millisecond, it's intuition that guides my voice. "That was a real nice sauna, boys, thanks for that!" I say in my best fake-friendly voice. They all bust up laughing, slapping one another on the back. The tension in the air dissipates like smoke in the wind. I stuff my shaking hands inside my pockets and take a long, deep breath.

Whew, it's over. For now.

I can't say for sure if the container incident was a warning, a none-too-discreet message to stop asking questions and mind my own business. I certainly took it as one. I remained friendly with those sketchy characters for the rest of my time in New York, but things were never quite the same after that, at least not for me. In retrospect, that was probably for the best. I wasn't going to join the mafia and hanging around the likes of made men, directly or indirectly, was going to get me into trouble eventually. Like Icarus flying too close to the sun, some things are better left untested.

It was with no small amount of relief that I closed the book on that part of my life.

Putting It Into Practice

As a child you probably looked up to adults because they were fearless (I know I did). From the vantage point of a six- or seven-year-old kid, a fully grown adult is like a demigod. They are the leaders, the indestructible ones, the prophets with a treasure trove of answers to life's inexplicable mysteries. But anyone that has ever crested their thirtieth birthday knows nothing could be further from the truth. As an adult you have only fractionally more answers than you did as a kid. And fear? You don't have less fear as you grow older, you have more! The world suddenly becomes a terrifying place. There are a million things to worry about when you get old: your posture, your spine, car insurance, muggings, economic crashes, toothaches, Halloween candy, and diabetes. The list goes on and on. Contrary to popular belief, there never comes a time in life where you wake up and outgrow your fear.

When I think about fear, my mind often drifts to boxers, specifically the greats like Mike Tyson. Talking about his psychological strategy for defeating opponents, Tyson famously said, *"I come out, I have supreme confidence - but I'm scared to death. I'm totally afraid. I'm afraid of every man, I'm afraid of losing, I'm afraid of being humiliated .... All during my training I've been afraid of this man...I've dreamed of him beating me. But once I'm in the ring, I'm a god. No one can beat me."*

It goes without saying that if "Iron Mike" Tyson feels fear before stepping into a ring, then it's pretty dang natural for the rest of us to share the burden.

I don't punch people for a living, nor do I think I would be any good at it if I tried. But I do have my share of fears. Aside from my work with Ocean Audit, my ocean freight auditing firm, I've been on nearly all of the major television networks and frequently give keynote speeches and presentations at conferences around the world. I'll tell you the truth: it never gets less scary. Every time I take the stage or sit down for an interview with a camera trained on me… whew… it's intense. I get that same choking feeling I had all those years ago locked inside of a big metal box in New York. There is always a moment, however brief, where the fear threatens to overtake me. Like Tyson on his walk into the ring, I am petrified. I am afraid of losing face, afraid of making a fool of myself, afraid of tripping over my words and stuttering. There are so many things that could possibly go wrong.

So, here's how I deal with fear in business.

Every time that ugly feeling rears its head at me, every time I feel like I am about to be yanked down by the weight of my own anxiety, I think about that incident in New York. I mentally go back and put myself into that shipping container. I smell the rusted metal and salty ocean air, and feel the blistering heat of that summer day. I remember the panicky realization that I might actually die in a soundless, airless, lightless box. I meditate on that feeling – sometimes for a few minutes, sometimes just for a few seconds, however long it takes. But when I come up for air, when I mentally relieve myself of that memory, I am light as a feather. Fear is all about perspective. It's terrifying to walk into a room full of board members and give a presentation about a bad quarter or missed Key

Performance Indicators (KPIs). But that experience becomes exponentially less terrifying when I compare it to speaking to an audience full of mafiosos, you know, people who might *actually* take my life for the wrong word or phrase.

Tim Ferriss, best-selling author of *The 4-Hour Workweek*, actually touches on this point in one of his more famous TED Talks. In fact, he even coined a name for the exercise: fear setting. In describing his own experiences combatting the lethargy of fear, Tim recalls:

"Then, one day, in my bliss of envisioning how bad my future suffering would be, I hit upon a gem of an idea. It was surely a highlight of my 'don't happy, be worry' phase: Why don't I decide exactly what my nightmare would be—the worst thing that could possibly happen as a result of my trip?

Well, my business could fail while I'm overseas, for sure. Probably would. A legal warning letter would accidentally not get forwarded and I would get sued. My business would be shut down, and inventory would spoil on the shelves while I'm picking my toes in solitary misery on some cold shore in Ireland. Crying in the rain, I imagine. My bank account would crater by 80% and certainly my car and motorcycle in storage would be stolen. I suppose someone would probably spit on my head from a high-rise balcony while I'm feeding food scraps to a stray dog, which would then spook and bite me squarely on the face. God, life is a cruel, hard bitch.

Then a funny thing happened. In my undying quest to make myself miserable, I accidentally began to backpedal. As soon as I cut through the vague unease and ambiguous anxiety by defining my nightmare, the worst-case scenario, I wasn't as worried about taking a trip. Suddenly, I started thinking of simple steps I could take to salvage my remaining resources and get back on track if all hell struck at once. I could always take a temporary bartending job to pay the rent if I had to. I could sell some furniture and cut back on eating out. I could steal lunch money from the kindergarteners who passed by my apartment every morning. The options were many. I realized it wouldn't be that hard to get back to where I was, let alone survive. None of these things would be fatal—not even close. Mere panty pinches on the journey of life.

I realized that on a scale of 1-10, 1 being nothing and 10 being permanently life-changing, my so-called worst-case scenario might have a temporary impact of 3 or 4. I believe this is true of most people and most would-be 'holy sh*t, my life is over' disasters."

- Tim Ferriss, 2017

Neither Tim nor myself are advocating that you find a mafia crew to clique up with or that you plunge into the world of extreme skydiving *sans parachute*. The point is not so much to seek out actual danger or to become an adrenaline junkie. The objective is to get comfortable with the feeling of fear. Learning how to live within that space while controlling your heartbeat and your breath will give you immense power: the power to *control your own reactions*! From a business perspective, this is one of the most highly sought-after skills in the world.

So, next time there's an opportunity that presents itself to you – the kind that makes you clamp down on your bladder so as not to pee your pants – I dare you to imagine something worse. Pull up a chair and sit down with that fear. Get good and cozy with it. Imagine all the things that could possibly go wrong, the absolute worst scenarios you can imagine. Got it figured out? Good. Now I want you to imagine how you would handle each and every one of those "life ending" disasters. Gun to your head, what would you do? How would you handle the pressure?

Though it might sometimes feel like it, nothing in business is really life or death.

My parting wisdom for you is this: client meetings aren't scary, the New York Mafia is. Put your fear into perspective, and get after your goals!

5 An Unfortunate Series of "Dates"

"Too often we underestimate the power of a touch, a smile, a kind word, a listening ear, an honest compliment, or the smallest act of caring, all of which have the potential to turn a life around."

Leo F. Buscaglia, *Living, Loving & Learning*

****

My professional career kept me bouncing around the continental U.S. like a corporate pinball, relocating every few months to a new city and a new sales hub within U.S. Lines. From 1982-1984, I was never in one place long enough to really make a home anywhere. The constant relocations, mildly perturbing though they were, paid off in full: I had become the number one ranked sales rep in the nation, not to mention the youngest. At twenty-three, I was running major divisions and closing some of the biggest numbers in our industry.

The thing you have to know about ocean freight sales, container sales, is that it has historically been an industry where big budgets prevail. An integral part of the selling process is the long-drawn-out foreplay that takes place over ten-course meals and limousine rides with prospective clients. Selling is very much like going on dates, like trying to seduce someone to get into business (not bed) with you. I was always encouraged to take clients out to boutique lunches, dinners, movies, and theater events. From the time I turned twenty-one until the day I founded my own business, I was constantly entertaining.

The result of this professional seduction was that I was left with the feeling that I had mastered the art of B2B relationships. The proof was in the pudding; I was closing more deals than anyone in the company and I was doing it in my characteristically eclectic style. One of my trade secrets was that I had an infallible system of completing intense research before each new business meeting. I would scour newspapers, media clippings, interviews, anything I could find about the person I was taking out. As a result, no two meetings were ever the same. I took pride in tailoring each and every one of my approaches to the communicative style that I thought this or that CEO would most appreciate. Find out what makes someone tick, leverage, and exploit that information, and then hook them with your sales proposition. That's what B2B relationships were to me back then. Until I moved to Dallas.

Dallas's Number One Recluse

Dallas proved to be a tough nut to crack. It wasn't the cowboys, the heat, or the cholesterol- heavy Texan diet: it was Jerry. In total, I only spent about a year in Dallas, but from my very first day, I had heard his name. The ocean shipping industry was small but productive in Texas, and so all of the industry professionals knew of one another on a first name basis. Often, at the end of an exhausting week, we'd get together at a local bar and trade battle stories from earlier on in the week. Almost without fail, someone would bring up the name Jerry. Usually, it was accompanied with an exasperated eye-roll, and a hearty pull from whatever the drink of choice was for the evening. Jerry was Dallas's most famous recluse, at least as far as ocean freight was concerned. The man had made his fortune importing enormous quantities of flowers which he transported via international cargo shipping. Thus, every sales rep within a hundred miles of the city was salivating at the prospect of bringing this big-ticket client on board. The problem was, Jerry didn't give a shit. He had absolutely no interest in the likes of salespeople, which I think he viewed as only slightly higher on the totem pole than male belly dancers or pet psychics. Every one told me flat out – there's no way to get to Jerry, don't even waste your time trying.

Challenge accepted.

Jerry became my personal mission and I spent months slowly edging my way into his circle. Maybe everyone's just been going about this the wrong way, I reasoned to myself. Maybe they just aren't grasping what this guy is really about. He was already a multimillionaire, so money wasn't his intrinsic motivation – he wasn't going to sign with me because I offered him the sweetest deal. His obstinacy in keeping his private world PRIVATE clued me into the fact that this was a man who cared about genuity and authenticity. If there was so much as a whiff of a sales pitch, he would spook. At the same time, there was no point in hiding who I was, either. A guy with that kind of resources at his disposal was certainly capable of doing his own "digging" and he'd find out I was a vendor in all of two seconds if I tried to keep it from him. So what does a guy like that want? What do you ask for when you can already buy everything you desire?

A protégé.

It seemed like sound logic – when you reach the pinnacle of success doesn't it stand to reason that what you really want is not the accolades, but rather someone to teach everything that you've learned? That's how I got Jerry to break his vow of silence. Instead of approaching him with promises of increased profits, revolutionized processes, or innovative shipping solutions, I just talked to him like a human being. I approached him with the attitude that I wanted to learn what had made him successful and to discern whether it was possible for someone else to replicate that success. As I said earlier, Jerry had the nose of a bloodhound when it came to bullshit and he could sniff out a disingenuous person a mile away. I think he recognized that I was serious, I was moldable, and I could be taught. Little by little, our relationship became more cordial and I could feel the walls crumble a day at a time.

When I finally worked up the nerve to invite him to dinner, I was more nervous than when I asked my high school date to prom. I was positive that he would tell me no, if he didn't just hang up on me first. Instead, he just shrugged casually and said okay. Sure, it was a bit anticlimactic, but I couldn't have cared less. I had work to do.

The night of our dinner, I made reservations at the richest, swankiest, over-the-top restaurant in Dallas. I would spare no expense, after all this was a man accustomed to luxury. There was just one more thing to do…I needed an extra layer of insulation, a cherry on top, something that would push him over the edge and right into the company's lap. My "wow factor" idea took shape in the form of a gigantic, custom made poster of one the company's ships stacked to the brim with multicolored containers. Underneath, the ingenious slogan read, "Keep them full." As in, please keep putting your damn containers on our ship because it's making us a whole heck of a lot of money.

In retrospect, the gesture strikes me as corny and exaggerated, exactly the opposite of Jerry's unassuming style. But it was too late to turn back now. Out walked the concierge with a framed photo of this colossal ocean freighter and those three neatly printed words. I was watching the look in his eyes like a hawk, studying every micro reaction. My powers of perception told me that the calculated gesture had landed flat on its ass. Jerry, though polite and gracious in accepting the poster, was none too impressed. "Thank you for the gift," he said a little dryly.

The rest of that night was bit more tense than usual and I was kicking myself for bringing that stupid picture in the first place. As one glass of wine turned to two, however, Jerry and his wife seemed to relax into the evening and our normal back-and-forth conversational tone seemed to resume. When it was time to call it a night, I ordered a limousine to drive Jerry and his wife back to their house. As he rose to leave, I handed him the picture frame which measured about 5.5 ft. long, with one single pane of glass covering the entire front. Whether it was my butterfingers or he didn't want the ugly thing in the first place, I'll never know. I watched in slow-motion horror as the frame slipped out of our hands and shattered brilliantly all over the sidewalk.

I tried frantically to regain control of the situation, rushing about collecting the warped pieces of the frame. "I, I, I, I'll get it fixed," I tried to choke out. Jerry just looked at me, held up his hand and said with solemn finality, "No, I'll take care of it." Now, I'm not superstitious, but if there was ever a moment where it seemed a bad omen had presented itself, this was it. Damn it! I had ruined it. I had ruined the whole thing trying to impress the guy instead of just being myself and going with what had already worked. I was devastated and sure that Jerry would most definitely think less of me somehow, and by extension, refuse to do business with U.S. Lines.

That was a major lesson for me: ninety-nine things had gone right, all the tiny details of the dinner had been planned flawlessly. Yet, all it took was one wrong turn – a silly accident – and the night had been ruined . But I was wrong about Jerry. He didn't look down on me, nor was he repulsed by our somewhat dramatic parting that evening. In fact, Jerry displayed a great deal of empathy and even reassured *me* that everything was fine. He bade me good night and told me to get home safely.

From that moment on, we conducted a very large number of mutually profitable transactions together. He took mercy on me when he didn't have to and I've never forgotten it.

The Most Expensive Bottle in the City

I found myself transferred once more to a major metropolitan city. With my Dallas days firmly behind me, my new bachelor pad was situated squarely in the Haight-Ashbury district of downtown San Francisco. Playfully steep hills, sunny golden days, and lots and lots of the devil's lettuce (marijuana) is what I remember about San Francisco. During the 80s, those prolific cross streets were a symbolic haven for Woodstock's forgotten children and my neighbors were more apt to be found sporting dreadlocks than pocket squares. I was doing the big city thing again, and loving every minute of it.

My success in the professional swooning of executives over dinner and drinks was no less effective in San Francisco. From the start, I found the clientele in the Bay Area to be, on the whole, more open and willing to hear my pitches. Before long, I was closing more than a few major accounts and had put that minor blip in Dallas behind me for good. Since I was frequenting the higher-end dining establishments on such a regular basis, I thought it would be wise to take a few courses on wine so that I might speak more intelligently about it over dinner with my clients. I was no sommelier, but by the end of the course I could split the hairs between a Chianti and Shiraz without looking like a total bonehead.

It was with this fragile confidence that I prepared for what would arguably be my most important meeting to date.

Mike Strubing was somewhere in his late forties and had amassed the considerable recognition owed to him as the very capable Vice President of Gap. Mike was the stereotype of the wildly successful CEO, the mold that all company men secretly (or not so secretly) aspire to be like someday. He was frequently involved in yacht club outings, celebrity fundraisers, and other philanthropic events throughout the city. We had spoken a few times and I felt confident that the rapport was mutual. Banking on this sentiment,

I asked him and his wife to join me for dinner one evening at the top of the Bank of America tower in San Francisco. The restaurant, it was widely circulated, was supposedly one of the best in the world (their menu prices certainly reflected that belief). It was a pristine glass box at the top of a skyscraper that afforded an unobstructed view of San Fran's twinkling lights.

Once again, I pulled no punches in trying to make a show of the evening; Mike and his wife were escorted to the restaurant in a private limousine paid for by yours truly. By the time we sat down at the table, I was already $1,000 into it. I scanned the wine menu looking for any safe ground, a bottle or brand that I might know so as to sound practiced and sophisticated. Unfortunately, the wine list could have been written in Cantonese for all that I was able to glean from it. Everything was imported from halfway around the world, and I didn't recognize any of the names. I had invited them out for dinner, and my instincts told me I should be the one that selected the wine for the table. Yet, when the waiter came over to ask for our selection, I was still frozen in a dyslexic fit, staring helplessly at the infinite vineyard varieties. In a moment absent my better judgement, I looked up and smiled across the table, "Mike, why don't you order the wine?"

As soon as the words were out of my mouth, I longed to take them back. Recalling the staggering prices of each bottle, I realized the gravity of my mistake: I had just given my guest the opportunity to order what might potentially be the most expensive bottle of wine in the city. I could very well blow my whole budget on this one dinner. I was frozen to my seat. Intuitively, Mike seemed to understand what was at stake. For just a moment, he gave me this mischievous look as if to say, "You're really going to leave it up to me, huh? Anything I want?" He skewered me for a moment longer with that Cheshire grin before composing himself. He looked up at the waiter and ordered a strong Cabernet – it was a $70 bottle. Relief coursed through me like hot soup on a wet, soggy day.

The waiter left, and Mike fixed his attention on me. "That could have been dangerous," he said, a smile tugging at the corner of his mouth again. I took a deep breath and looked him in the eye. "I trust you," I said.

He had the perfect opportunity to be an asshole; heck, I had served it to him on a golden platter. If he had ordered ten filets and the most expensive bottle of wine, I would have paid it all right then and turned in my resignation the next day. But he didn't. He did the right thing. He showed me mercy when he could have taken advantage of me.

The Stuttering CEO

You win some, you lose some. Everybody knows that's just part of the game. Sure, I had sales talent, no two ways about it. But, I'd also been saved by sheer luck and the moral uprightness of decent human beings more than my fair share of times. The incident in the Bank of America tower notwithstanding, I was crushing San Francisco and driving some seriously impressive numbers. What small losses I had encountered, I took on the chin and did my best to learn from. In the meantime, the boozing and tail-kissing continued.

Actually, there is one meeting in particular that stands out to me from this chapter in my life. One beautiful, sunny afternoon I called up a new prospective client, another big hitter in the shipping industry - we'll call him Paul. So, I called Paul up and invited him to lunch with me. "Hey Paul, Steve Ferreira here. I was thinking you and I could go grab a bite to eat tomorrow at this Italian place I've been hearing a lot about...". We had a delightful conversation on the phone and I knew this was going to be an easy sell. Paul and I hit it off right from the start. He agreed to come to lunch with me the following day and told me the restaurant was delicious and actually right next to his office. "Perfect," I said, "I can swing by and pick you up around 11:45." He told me he was looking forward to it, and we left things at that. Though we had never met in person, I felt no anxiety about this meeting. I could already tell that this guy and I were going to see eye to eye.

So the next morning I go to pick him up from his office.

He gets in the car, shakes my hand, and everything's going great. He was a regular-looking guy, nice enough, though not necessarily someone that would stand out in any noticeable way if you saw him walking down the street. As we're meandering through the lunchtime traffic, I notice that Paul is not saying very much. Actually, he's not saying anything at all. I'm lobbing feelers out left and right and not one of them is hitting the mark. I can't figure out what's going on. We had great rapport on the phone, what's got this CEO all clammed up now that he's in the car with me? I mentally shrug it off, some people just don't like to talk in the car I guess.

I park the car and we walk into the restaurant; our table for two is reserved in a private little back corner of the joint. The waiter sets the menus down on the table and then disappears into the background to give us some time. At that moment, something happens to Paul. I can see his face twist into a kind of strange grimace, it's as if the man's got shooting back pain or something that he doesn't want me to know about. He's only spoken all of about seven words since I picked him up. "Paul, are you feeling alright? You don't look so good," I asked as gently as I could. Whatever veneer of control he was holding onto collapsed underneath the weight of that one question.

As it turns out, when Paul gets nervous he suffers from a debilitating stutter. I'm not talking about a mild Elmer Fudd stutter, either. Paul has the kind of stutter that makes him choke on the words "chicken soup" for a full five minutes before the poor guy can get it out.

I'm floored.

At this point, I have absolutely no idea what to do. Paul is a mess, clearly embarrassed and ashamed, the more so because he gave no indication of his condition over the phone. For my part, I'm squirming in my chair like there's a bed of hot coals beneath me. My instincts are telling me to abandon ship, to get out of here while I still can. There's no way this guy is going to want to do business together after this, I'm thinking to myself. I'm watching his face turn redder and redder as the spit collects at the corner of his mouth, all the words strangled somewhere in the back of his throat. This is not how I imagined the meeting going. All at once, however, I'm hit with a series of memories like a brick shithouse. I'm thinking of Jerry, when I smashed his ridiculously ornate picture frame and how gracious and cool he played it. I'm thinking about Mike and the way he could have buried me with that tab over dinner. But he didn't. He did the right thing. I'm thinking about all the other people in my life that have led with compassion and empathy in their business.

Without thinking too much about it, I lean over the table and gently put my hand on the small of Paul's arm. With my other hand I politely motion for him to stop his contorted efforts at further speech for a moment. He takes a deep gulp of air. "Take your time," I said, as I looked him right in the eye. "You're safe here. There's no rush at all, okay? Everything's all right." It was a surreal moment, and I could see the tears welling up in his eyes as he just nodded at me. He understood. I wasn't going to judge him, I wasn't going to run away or slander his reputation in bar room stories with the boys later on that evening. I meant every word that I said to him, he was safe.

He stuttered through the entire rest of the meal, speaking only with great difficulty. Afterwards, he went on to become one of my best customers.

Putting It Into Practice

I am of the mind that you could make a strong case that the generation growing up now has it even harder than I did back in my day. The all-seeing eye that is social media has propagated a movement, a cultural transition, towards the pursuit of an unrealistic standard of perfection that is extremely damaging. Not even the ostrich with its head firmly buried in the sand is excused from the collective judgement passing and social crusades that saturate the web. Our children, like it or not, are being exposed to a type of digital, constructed interaction in which they are judged every minute of every day for what they look like, what they wear, and how they speak. There is no safe place to hide anymore, no zone of quiet obscurity. All of us are being dragged into the light with our pants down.

When I reflect on my career, and the experiences mentioned above, I can't help but become poignantly aware of the degradation of values taking place right in front of our eyes. This past year has already ushered in some of the most sweeping global challenges our world has faced in recent years, and I think it's fairly safe to assume we are not out of the water yet. The next generation of business owners, entrepreneurs, and CEOs are going to face a level of crisis that most of us have never been exposed to before. And that worries me.

Our universities raise their educational standards every year. We have brilliant students, and graduates that are making incredible changes in the world. But, I wonder. Beyond the accounting classes, and supply chain analyses, and case study breakdowns, who is teaching our next generation of leaders to be empathetic, to communicate with a high degree of emotional intelligence? What was once relegated to the perfunctory and uninspiring title of "soft skills," is only now beginning to be recognized as the backbone of all business relationships. That is to say, who is priming the next generation of innovators to lead with an empathetic, humane first step?

My expertise, ocean freight shipping and invoicing, is in a niche industry. At its core, however, what I do – what I have always done – is build and foster relationships. People are the foundation of my business, they are what keeps everything else afloat. I've never lost sight of that. As a company leader, it's paramount to my success that I approach each and every professional relationship with the patience and unerring dedication of a new parent. Some days, I accomplish this more readily than others. However, my intention is always to go out into the world and bring with me a state of empathy, understanding and authenticity.

So, here are my thoughts.

Given the choice, I would rather have in my hands a list of ten, unfailingly loyal clients, partners, associates, etc., rather than a treasure trove of 1,000 unprimed leads. The truth is, I am confident from that list of ten names that I could draw more value, more revenue, and more satisfaction than if I cold-called all 1,000 strangers. Business is about relationships. I'll say it again – *business is about relationships*! We are living through a digital transformation, a key moment in history, and it's becoming almost too easy to allow technology to take the place of meaningful human interactions. If you're finding that your business is underperforming, your conversion rates sagging, I challenge you not to look outwardly for a software solution or a product reinvention. Instead, I would advise you to take stock of your professional relationships. How well have you maintained them? How often do you check in with your clients about matters that have nothing to do with business? How often do you make them feel seen and heard?

That's the not-so-secret sauce.

Lead with empathy. Lead with compassion. Lead with gratitude. You want the recognition of being a powerful leader in your space? Give, give, and then give some more. Make it a mission that when people are talking to you, they feel they are the only person in your universe. Give them every ounce of your attention, and like gravity, let the rest work itself out naturally.

Our children, the leaders of tomorrow, are watching. What will we show them by way of example?

6 Losing My Mind: The Seedy Underbelly of the Orient

"Richard, you're a tough guy," I began.

"You've had your passport taken away by the government, several of your fingers cut off by the mafia… I bet people don't say no to you often, do they? But I am saying no. I am not going to reduce the price you pay for your ocean containers."

His beady little black eyes made my blood turn cold. Without so much as a word, his look seemed to tell me, "Ferreira – he never called me by my first name – Ferreira, I could make you disappear so easily. So, so very easily." Tense and unmoving as granite, I waited for his reaction.

He squinted at me from across the table before inclining his glass of amber Chivas in my direction. I tentatively slugged back my own mouthful of spiced whiskey to calm the nerves. Calamity had been averted…at least for now.

****

In the mid 1980s, Taiwan was a steaming metropolis of prostitution, organized crime, and illegal drug smuggling. Taipei had been my home for two years, and it drew the nefarious characters of the greater Chinese underworld like 1920s New York drew immigrants with the promise of a better life. At twenty-eight, it was my first overseas promotion and a real taste of professional autonomy. Heading the division of Sea Land's, an ocean freight company, Europe-to-Taiwan ocean freight division would prove to be the most challenging, chaotic, and exhilarating position I would hold within the company.

I settled into my flat at the Berlin Building in Tianmu, a ritzy part of Taipei, in 1988. My first order of business was to find my right-hand man, a Chinese counterpart that could help me navigate the linguistic and cultural barriers inherent in international business. After some digging, I found William, a great man of small stature who made up for any deficiency in height with an astounding work ethic and great knowledge of the Asian to European trade market. His only flaw was that William had a strange propensity for wearing blue suits with bleached white socks (I never did find the nerve to tell him myself, so I asked one of my assistants to pass along the message). When I stood up at a conference in Taiwan and told one hundred customers what we were going to do together as a team to get them strong wins in their businesses, I commanded the room in English. Immediately after, I would turn it over to William who would light up the room in Mandarin. We were a kick-ass team from day one.

If William was my work wife in Taiwan, then John was everything else – my driver, my bodyguard, my confidant, and my bartender. Officially, John was my full-time driver and ex-Chinese army protector. He slogged through the traffic of downtown Taipei twice a day, bringing me to and from the office in a Japanese kit car assembled in Taiwan. John and I seemed to have that type of synchronistic communication that required no more than a few eyebrow wags to get a message across. Pretty soon, we fell into a routine: John would pick me up from the office in the late afternoon as the sun began dipping below the lush vegetation of the mountains. In the back seat, waiting for me ever so patiently, would always be two ice cold Taiwanese pijo (beer). I would crack the top off the first one while I worked my way through emails and telefax orders in the middle of rush hour traffic. When we finally arrived home, I was "on call" the rest of the night, clubbing, drinking, and taking clients out to massage parlors. It was a general cacophony of bad habits that messed with my head. Through it all, though, there was John. He drove us around to do a lot of strange shit in Taipei, and I never wavered in my respect for him.

Those two years were a kaleidoscopic blur of alcohol, red light districts, teacups, massage parlors, and endless hours on the job. I was having the time of my life, going rogue out there in the Far East. As a young, single kid in his late twenties, I was banking a hundred percent of my salary and living exclusively off the "hardship pay" – yes, Taiwan was considered a hardship back then. To be fair, there was always a heightened state of anxiety. Armed soldiers were posted on every street corner, edgy from the omnipresent threat that was mainland China. Between the drinks and the endlessly revolving door of dates, it was a fantastic struggle to keep the names of all the characters straight. I was living a VIP lifestyle that would have given any Jordan Belfort types (*The Wolf of Wall Street*) a run for their money. But Taiwan could be a cruel mistress and she loved only two things: money and pleasure.

Both were bound to take their toll eventually.

Taiwanese Tough Guys

From the time I stepped foot on that island in the East China Sea, I was in mafia territory and I knew it. The initial public broadcast about my intentions to open up the Asian-European ocean freight market did not fall on deaf ears. Word spread quickly that there was a new American player on the scene, one with access and opportunity to make some serious waves. It didn't take long, then, for the Taiwanese mob to make their introductions.

Richard Liu was the regional head of the Taiwanese mob. Not the boss or even the underboss, but something like a captain, with enough authority to command respect from everyone within his orbit. He was a legitimate freight forwarder. He just also happened to belong to an enterprising group of individuals that specialized in removing your appendages. Good old Richard. Moral apprehensions aside, Richard was an ocean freight client of mine, and as such I was always on the periphery of the more dangerous crowds in Taipei. I would often be out to dinner with him and his associates, and while a bit tense at times, I'd be lying if I said they weren't good company. Those Taiwanese tough guys were an endless source of entertainment with their petty squabbling, posturing, and generally riotous behavior when drinking. Every once and a while, though, something would kick off. An incident would happen, and I would be reminded that I was indeed walking a very tight line.

One night, I was out to dinner with a client and we were finishing another lavish meal before heading home. He was a middle-aged American man with a Chinese wife who happened to be extremely well-connected to the female side of the mafia's business. I had heard through the grapevine that there had been some trouble in one of their dealings lately, but the man didn't bring it up at dinner and I honestly did not think to ask. After we paid the check and stood up to leave, he offered to drive me home. We had both drunk a considerable amount of alcohol and I thought it best just to call (my driver) John for a ride. But the man was insistent; he'd take me home. I got in his Mercedes and he meandered through the winding roads of the city until he dropped me off at my home, without incident. I bade him goodnight and promptly fell into a dreamless alcoholic slumber.

The next day, he turned up dead. Murdered.

It was a bad real estate deal, or so I heard it said later on. The man had failed in his fiduciary responsibilities and paid the price for it. Though I could never confirm, the whispers in the teahouses and massage parlors all pointed to his wife; she had put the hit out, which ultimately ended his life. Maybe it was selfish, maybe not, but I couldn't stop thinking about how that guy had driven me home. He was in my driveway… if they were following him then….that could have been me. Suddenly, the chummy relationships I had developed with Richard and his boys seemed a whole hell of a lot less certain.

A week or so later I met the widow at his funeral. She shook my hand and looked me dead in the eye. She was a former go-go dancer turned hardened alpha female. She was like one of the femme fatale movie villains out of a James Bond film, with her long, red, dragon nails. She had that awesome command over her own power, such that if she just looked at you the wrong way, your manhood crawled up inside you. She was that vicious.

After her husband's death, she took over the company. I began to think maybe that was the grand design all along. It goes without saying that his killers were never found.

The Little Black Book of Sin

Regardless of what my title said on paper, my capacity in Taiwan was that of a professional entertainer. My naturally outgoing personality made me the perfect candidate for wining and dining some of Sea Land's most prestigious clients.

I would arrive at the Taipei airport and scoop up that week's MVP and deliver him promptly to the YY Steakhouse for a carnivorous, culinary extravaganza. We'd jostle back and forth with some small talk and interesting anecdotes about life in Taipei while we gorged ourselves on wine and seared meat. The whole time, however, I'd be sizing up the person, trying to figure them out. You know, it was like trying to evaluate and predict a storm before it happened. What kind of guy was this? Did he expect some womanizing? Was he the massage parlor type that would be looking for a little something "extra" this evening? Or did he want to hit the hay early and be up at the crack of dawn to drive some balls down the fairway? Unfortunately, the latter were few and far between.

Anticipating the needs and desires of my clients became something like an art form. As I became more and more practiced, I amassed what became the ultimate little black book of sin. By the time I left Taipei in 1990, there were few mamasans at the massage parlors that didn't know me on a first-name basis. The business executives that came to visit me on the grounds of professional networking were not ignorant of Taiwan's reputation for an after-hours good time. Moreover, they weren't at all shy about expressing their (**cough cough**) carnal desires. As the ambassador of my company, I was expected to bend over backwards to make these guys happy. And so I did.

Enter the Lucky Star.

The Lucky Star club seemed to exist within its own dimension, somewhere beyond that of time, space, and human morality. Once inside, you traded air for a thick wall of scent comprised of $3 perfume and cigarettes. Its bright flashing lights danced off the mirrored tables in such a way that you were constantly dizzy, or on the point of an epileptic fit. Liquor sales from the bar were the legitimate arm of Lucky Star's business, but its owners weren't burdened by the notion of discretion. After ushering my client into a comfortable, nondescript booth, the madam of the house would send over five or six "bar girls" for our entertainment. Each one oozed sexuality and had their own litany of practiced compliments in English. The madam eyed us like a hawk the whole time, cataloging every detail. After running up a tab several hundred dollars long, she would coquettishly suggest that perhaps it was time for some…comfort. I declined but was, of course, expected to front the bill for my client.

It was a magical place; an adult, Chinese Disneyland on steroids.

At the height of my corporate debauchery, I was spending somewhere in the ballpark of $2,000 a week (keep in mind this was back in 1988) on entertainment, food, and drinks. To the outside observer, I was living the dream. I had money, a certain degree of power and respect, autonomy, etc. But the pressure and the unhealthy environment were closing in on me. I was in a doctor's office at least once a week from fatigue, getting B-12 energy booster shots, working ninety hours a week, and drinking my weight in alcohol. I slept little and dined out often. At one point, I had sort of a mental breakdown and remember crying on the bathroom floor, thinking to myself, "I can't take this shit for another two years." Between the mafia, the drugs, the girls, and the booze – it was all the way too. And Sea Land knew it.

When I finally rotated out of Taiwan in 1990 to a different assignment, my bosses at Sea Land informed me I had lasted six months longer than anyone else at the Taipei posting. It was like some sort of Jason Bourne experience; my superiors knew that the max anyone could handle this type of pressure was two years. Any longer than that and they inevitably cracked. In reconciliation, they said, "Hey, how about a change of scenery, a move to Hong Kong?" Well, what the hell, I thought to myself. Why not?

You might think that skipping over the pond to that other tropical Asian island would be just as erratic and stress inducing. In reality, there was no comparison; Hong Kong was strawberries and whipped cream. Crazy as it seems, after one year of "boring" club dinners with expats and Americans diplomats, my mind would sometimes wander and I'd catch myself thinking, "Maybe those Taipei strip clubs really weren't so bad after all." Then again, twenty-twenty hindsight.

Getting Dumped – Sort Of

Taiwan and Hong Kong were, respectively, a roller coaster of emotions that took me to my breaking point and back. It was the most money I had ever made, and from a professional standpoint, the hands-on experience accumulated was beyond measure. In truth, I probably never would have left had it been up to me. Unfortunately, it was not.

In 1992, Sea Land hired an outside consultancy to conduct a case study of how we might cut our overhead costs and improve the cushioning of our margins. The consultants pointed their fingers at Asia and said, "Start there." At the time, there were about thirty-forty expats living in Asia, which was a considerable number for a company the size of Sea Land. All of us were making good money and blowing an exorbitant amount of our budgets on business dinners and after hours executive parties. That said, it would have been a cataclysmic blow to the company if they had simultaneously removed all of the foreign reps from their stations. They decided to keep only ten. It was deemed the best course of action to let the local talent get promoted and simply run a leaner operation.

Time to bring the other thirty expats back home.

I had been putting in well over eighty hours a week for four straight years. Maybe I was a bit beat up and in need of a vegetable or two, but aside from that, I felt like Superman. As the youngest expat ever promoted to a foreign post, I was untouchable. I had these grandiose visions that in the not-too-distant future I would be running the company, pulling the strings on the global market. It never crossed my mind, not even for a moment, that they might cut the cord. It just didn't make sense to me. If I had been insubordinate, or gone above my superiors in an act of childish impudence, I could have understood the "demotion." But it came out of nowhere; my life, as I knew it, was over.

The only thing I can liken it to is your very first kiss. You work up the nerve to go over to the girl you've been crushing on for some time. You march on over, present yourself before this girl and - BAM! The whole universe is working in conjunction with you; the girl kisses you back. It's amazing! It's everything you thought it would be! It's the entire cosmos in alignment with your plans, and then *poof*…some overzealous school chaperone pulls you two apart, right in the middle of your best fantasy. No closure whatsoever.

That's what it felt like to me. Only, in this case, it was that management study that was acting like a chaperone, absolutely killing my vibe.

I was determined to see the situation in a positive light, however. Okay, so I was going back home, but heck! I was definitely going to be a regional Vice President or something of the sort. I'd be closer to corporate headquarters as well which would up my chances for promotion. Yeah, maybe it wasn't looking so bad after all, I reasoned. That idea dropped like a stone from my mind when they hit me with, "Well, I don't think there is really much available right now, but you can just be a salesperson. We actually have an opening in Cleveland, Ohio."

Cleveland, fucking, Ohio. That was the offer.

There was one, and only one, silver lining from how that experience ended: it taught me the value of having a contingency plan. One subtle thing I started to take note of while working for Sea Land abroad was the sheer volume of bogus invoices in ocean freight shipping. Everywhere you looked, there was a surplus charge for this or that misstep, a piece of arbitrary red tape that could sometimes amount to thousands of dollars in penalties. Companies would just bend over and pay to make them go away.

Without having a definite plan in mind, I started accumulating documents and artifacts that I believed were not righteous.

In other words, let's say that it was my company and I noticed a billing discrepancy for a customer that amounted to a $10,000 penalty. Sometimes this happened because the ship, and subsequently the cargo, didn't arrive on time and the boat had to be moored longer. Well, in an instance like that, I would pick up the phone and call some individual on the other side of the world and vehemently protest the stupidity of the charge. Nine times out of ten, I would get it waived, and the client was overjoyed.

As situations like this continued to happen, I became aware that these were not simply isolated incidents; there was a consistent pattern of overbilling in the freight shipping industry. All these extra fees and charges were invoiced by hand, and they were different each time. Because ocean freight is such a niche business, there are very few experts who understand the ins and outs of the international legalities. One week the client invoice might be $3,000; the very next week, the same item would be $3,300 with no explanation given. Even to folks with more than just a tacit understanding, these invoices were intimidating. The receipt was no grocery bill; each invoice could be hundreds of lines long. Plenty of room for someone to sneak in a hundred dollars here, a hundred dollars there. It added up over time, and I kept track of every penny.

In accumulating all these invoices, which amounted to physical evidence of the hundreds and thousands of dollars I'd saved my clients in refunds over the years, an idea was slowly turning in my mind. By the time I left Hong Kong and returned stateside, my little collection had turned into a sizable book. What I had in my hands, though I did not yet know it, would later become the foundation for my own business. I would use my collection and my rigorously documented experiences to create a case study/proof of concept to leverage with my future clients. Look, I'd say to them, this is my track record. This is what I've been able to do in the past, and I guarantee I can do the same for you or I won't charge you a thing.

I won't lie to you, though. I felt a little torn. Regardless of how unceremoniously I'd been cycled back stateside, Sea Land had put tremendous faith in me, and without them I would never have been promoted to Taiwan. I wanted to strike out on my own and start this new business, but there was a nagging voice in my head that said I owed them. In my mind, it was a matter of loyalty and honor. So I made a compromise with myself: I wouldn't leave the company just yet, but I also was not going to give up on my business idea, either. I just couldn't resist.

I stayed up into the wee hours of the night, writing the business plan for what eventually became my first breakaway entrepreneurial venture. After two or three years of consistent work, I finally felt that the time had come: I was ready to move on to greener pastures. Quietly, well under the radar, I began making plans to resign, to pull the plug and try my hand at the table. To this day, I cannot recall the exact sequence of events. Somehow, my business plan was leaked. And so it happened one morning that I was called into the senior VP's office, without a hint of pretense or warning. Even though I was already on my way out, I couldn't help the perspiration gathering under my arms and in the palms of my hand as I strode into that pristine office. This is it, I thought. I'm going to get fired. Well, first I'm going to get royally chewed out, and then I'm going to get fired. What if they accuse me of wasting company resources or abusing corporate assets? There could be a lawsuit… or worse…

My head was swimming.

The senior VP brings me into his office, and the man is about as smiley and warm as a cactus. He's gunning for the world's best poker face, and damned if he isn't right up there with the best of them. I couldn't get a read at all. I made up my mind right then; I'm just going to tell them the truth, everything. I'm going to be honest and lay it all on the line. So I did exactly that. I told him in my most professional voice, "This is the business plan I'm working on. This is what I want to do, and this is how I plan to get there, etc., etc." When I finished, I looked up, internally bracing for impact. I was ready to get thrown out of the office, ready to get screamed at and talked down to. I was ready for anything, except what actually happened.

This man, who up until this point had not seemed capable of contorting his face into a smile, did just that. He smiled at me and said, "Well, why don't we be your incubator then?" That just floored me. I literally could not process what he'd said for a moment and asked him to clarify what he meant. "Well," he began, "how would you feel about running your own business, but running it internally within the corporate organization?" I couldn't believe it. They were giving me the chance to run my company as a unit within Sea Land, a Fortune 500 company. And that wasn't all.

"Not only do we want you to run it," he continued, "but if you run it successfully for three years, we'll give you a six-figure bonus." *What the hell had just happened? Was I dreaming all this?* I was perplexed, overjoyed, and relieved all at the same time. The truth is, even Sea Land recognized the value of my idea. They wanted a piece of the pie and, in return, they were offering a sizable safety net. It took me all of half a second to agree. I signed a three year non-compete agreement and used their existing framework to test the viability of my own business.

I was finally doing the entrepreneurial thing, and I was doing it on their dime.

Putting It Into Practice

Living and working in Taiwan was one of the most memorable experiences of my professional life. The endless variety of obstacles and characters I faced sharpened my B2B skills to such an extent that it primed me to a near perfect state of readiness to start my own business. That said, it also took a tremendous toll on my mental and physical health. While I chalked a great deal of it to the "lifestyle," in actuality I was burning the candle dangerously close to both ends. By proxy, my company had put in me contact with some very dangerous individuals and situations that could have meant death or serious injury. For all my dedication and profitable outcomes in Taiwan, when the time came, I was pulled out like a dead battery.

While the experience was extremely jarring to live through, it taught me an incredible lesson: _Never ever give all you have in pursuit of someone else's dream_. You can put in eighty hour work weeks, bust your ass, lose your physical and mental health, only to find out that your company deems you replaceable. If you're going all in, it better be for your own dream. Now, I'm not advocating that everyone go out and quit their jobs. You have to make a living somehow. I'm also not in favor of doing half-ass work, or not giving each project your absolute full attention. But it is possible to do both of these things while keeping your eyes peeled for opportunities to create your own contingency business.

Here's what I recommend:

1. **Learn a process/pattern while you are working for someone else.**

   Regardless of what industry you are in, there are always going to be patterns, and within those patterns, weak points. Once you've identified the area, figure out how to test those holes for their efficacy. Are they always present or do the mistakes/problems seem to fluctuate? In my experience, the shipping industry was beautifully reliable in its greediness. Figure out how to break the pattern and then put it back together (e.g., how do I solve the problem after I've pinpointed it?). Once you are able to do that – congratulations, you've got your business idea! Remember, selling is never really about "selling," it's about providing a solution to a problem. And if your would-be client is currently unaware of that problem, well, all the better for you.

2. **When at all possible, use other people's money as a litmus test**.

If you find a hole in the business, offer your company the solution and see if it works. Use the massive budgets of a corporate body to test your theory on the micro level so that you can later apply it to the macro. Keep detailed notes, and document the entire process. If you are able to fix the problem consistently, you know that you have found a real opportunity. If you find your hypothesis isn't up to snuff, you didn't lose any of your own money in the process, and you still get the recognition of going after innovative strategies to improve your company's efficiency. Win-win.

3. **Your company uses you, so use them right back.**

   Employment should be a mutually beneficial relationship. Actively seek out trainings, seminars, and company-sponsored events where you can acquire new skills and information. You can be sure that your company wants to use every available joule of your energy; consider looking at them the same way. What programs or opportunities can you use for self-development? How can you organically grow your professional network? You never know when these commodities might prove invaluable down the road.

4. **Nihilism just might save your career.**

   Assume that you are going to be phased out. Assume that the company will go under. Assume that you have to start over, right now, from scratch. What would you do? An attitude saturated with pessimistic outlooks is neither helpful nor advisable. However, many people fail to even *consider* the prospect of calamity until it plants a big sloppy kiss on their lips (*ahem – COVID-19*). Don't be that person. Even when things are going good, the pragmatic entrepreneur in you should be scouting for the next available S-curve. You will never regret having a backup plan in place should you someday find that you need to make a quick exit. I promise you, it's absolutely worth the investment of your time.

7 From the Penthouse to the Basement

If your ninth grade English class was anything like mine, I'd wager you were subjected to the long-winded storytelling of a certain Greek blind man. Specifically, I am thinking of Homer and his epic *Odysseus*. I'd be lying if I said I was a premier fanboy of Greek mythology, but there was one story from that hefty poem that has stayed with me: the tale of the lotus eaters. It goes something like this:

****

"After an irascible and bloody campaign at Troy, Odysseus and his men set out to embark on the long journey homeward in their twelve, stout wooden ships. Before long, however, a great and powerful storm threatened to capsize their fleet, dragging it to the bottom of the Aegean. Odysseus commanded his men to moor their ships at a nearby island, a place where they might find refuge to wait out the tempestuous sea.

Upon landing on the mysterious island, he sent a scouting party of twenty men, led by Eurylochus, to go in search of food and water. Hours passed and still the men did not return. Worried for the fate of his comrades, Odysseus himself decided to lead a search party of fifty to find their missing crew.

After hours of fruitless wandering, the men finally achieved their aim – they found the crew. Rather than a scene of barbarity and violence, as one might have expected, the twenty men of the original search party were complacently strewn about a beautiful pool of water, gorging themselves on a strange fruit of the lotus with the native inhabitants of the island. Unharmed though they appeared, each of the soldiers showed no sign of recognition towards their commander. In fact, all seemed to be lost in a state of blissful, drugged torpor.

Noticing this, Odysseus commanded his men not to eat the fruit which the strange inhabitants of the island had provided. Forcefully, he gathered this miscreant twenty and dragged them, hand over foot, back to the beach and the rest of the fleet. "Tie them up!" he ordered. And so each man that had tasted the fruit was lashed to the boat, still in a state of confusion and delirium.

Slowly, one by one, the bound men regained their senses. Their eyes cleared as the fog within their minds lifted. As they looked up and about, they recognized the face of Odysseus and were ashamed. Had it not been for his rescue, they would have left behind their comrades, their families and their homes. They would have given up everything they held dear, all because of a tempting little fruit…"

Homer, Odyssey

****

In 1997, the universe aligned in such a way as to present me with its own tempting little lotus fruit. I had been a business owner for just over three years and had proudly watched as the ruminations of my professional fantasy took hold; my business was alive, well, and turning no small profit. I was doing it. I had struck out on my own, leaving Sea Land behind, and was fulfilling that greatest of capitalistic dreams: entrepreneurialism. I was swollen with pride and excited at the prospects of my future. After my initial success was proven to be more than just a fluke, I started attracting the attention of some major corporations in the industry. They started out soft, throwing small feelers and jabs, trying to determine my willingness to sell. Eventually, I was approached by one of these corporations and asked point blank if I'd be willing to part with the business, to the tune of $1M.

At thirty-seven years old, one million dollars epitomized success to me. It was the ultimate dangling carrot, the perfect lotus, and I jumped at the opportunity with both hands. Before I could even take stock of my feelings, I had signed away all I had worked for. Almost immediately there was a crushing sense of regret. I'd buckled too early. A wave of emptiness rushed in to fill the place where my business had once lived. Call it postpartum depression, but it had, after all, been my baby for over three years. I'd eaten, worked, and slept every moment of the last thirty-six months with this one, singular idea. It was mine… and then it was gone.

At least there was the million dollars, I rationalized. Even in my strange funk I realized that there were definitely worse positions to find oneself in. So, I did what any other irresponsible young man might have done; I set off to spend extravagantly, or die trying.

And spend, I did.

Money *Can* Buy Happiness – at Least for a While

So there I was, a thirty-seven year old, in Seattle a gainfully unemployed bachelor. Now, I don't care what anybody says, there are a lot of interesting ways you can spend your money if you've got a million dollars and some time to kill. I'll be damned if one of them isn't going to make you happy. At least for a while.

At the beginning, I sort of eased myself into things. I started waking up later in the day, and taking a more relaxed approach to my diet and exercise (like eating raw cookie dough with a spoon). I was also a regular at any number of the high-end bars in downtown Seattle and frequently burned the midnight oil, sipping cocktails and talking marketing with the owners. Other times, I'd just wander aimlessly around the city at night like some sort of benevolent ghost. Somewhere in the blur of those first few months, I decided to pursue my second great love: golf. Roll your eyes all you want, but I've always found there to be something positively cathartic about smacking old whitey down the fairway. The long hours of solitude under a cloudless blue sky. The smell of fresh cut grass and the cute little golf girls in their…nevermind.

Anyway, since I was now a man of some means, I devoted all that restless energy into my new dream: becoming a PGA pro. Singapore, the Philippines, Mexico, Paris, Colombia… between 1997 and 2000, you name the exotic locale and I was probably there playing golf. I spent hundreds of thousands of dollars on lessons and memberships, custom-made clubs and massages, anything to improve my game. I even saw a hypnotist at one point to help with my golf swing. I can't say I saw much improvement, but we did end up dating for a while.

With the unshakeable focus of a monk, my golf game steadily improved. I was getting damn good, and yet… for all that, I couldn't shake the realization that less than one percent of even the most talented golfers ever make it to the pros. In other words, golf was anything but a sure-fire opportunity to make money. Given the way I was spending, I'd need some sort of backup plan, and fast.

I made the "strategic" decision to invest a few hundred thousand dollars into founding my next company, Pink Golf. Essentially, Pink was designed to educate female executives on how to conduct business on the golf course with their male colleagues. It might sound a bit strange today, but the idea didn't just come out of nowhere. In 1997, Seattle was Microsoft country all the way and there were hundreds of senior executive women who worked within its larger apparatus. It was considered an important rite of initiation that they knew how to play, and play well at that, against their male counterparts. These women wanted the private lessons and education to improve themselves, both professionally and within the confines of the sport. I knew I was good at golf, but where I really excelled was in communication. So, I hired a female professional golfer and together we ran Pink Golf for three years. Unfortunately, from an investment standpoint, it was more or less a bust. Looking back, I chalk up most of that time to the category of pro bono work (more on that later).

I'll remind the reader that at this point in my life, I was very much a bachelor. As a result, I was something of a serial dater as well. I was comfortable around women but I hadn't really found anyone, as of yet, that made me consider a serious future. Being around those female executives, though…it had a great impact on my social life. If I wasn't spending money on golf, I certainly found other, more voluptuous avenues to deplete my bank account.

Before I knew it, I became Tiffany's favorite customer. I was the epitome of new money, buying random girlfriends diamond necklaces and first class tickets to resorts around the world. When things didn't work out with the hypnotist, I met my insurance agent and we started dating for a time. When that, too, came to its inevitable conclusion, I hopped on a flight to Paris where I met a Lebanese woman who I had a brief on-again, off-again relationship with. Just to show her there were no hard feelings at the end, I bought her a diamond tennis bracelet.

I was spending like it came from a bottomless well, and as far as I was concerned, it did.

90 Day Fiancé in Real Life

I arrived in Prague riding the coattails of my three year extravaganza but looking, and feeling, like a husk of my former self. Unabated hedonism takes its toll. What's more, unfortunate turns in the stock market and my personal investments had leveled my savings to nothing. By the time I stepped off that international flight into the cold Czech winter, I was nearly 100k in debt. My fleeting hopes at becoming a golf professional were all but squashed by then and I was in a strange state of mind. My life seemed to have lost all sensible direction. I was once again a stranger in a strange land. I didn't know it at the time, but I was about to meet the love of my life.

Serendipity, that's what comes to mind.

Back then, she was a beautiful stranger walking down the street towards me. I stopped to ask her for directions, my face half buried against the wool of my coat, as I tried unsuccessfully to duck the biting winter cold. She gave me that half startled, half amused look that women give men when they feel they've seen this trick done before. The, "*Seriously? That's the best you could come up with?"* type of look. But it wasn't a ploy, I was one genuinely lost American wandering the streets of Prague, alone. We stood there shuffling in the cold for a few minutes while I talked her up. She seemed to come into focus more and more with each passing moment. She was stunning, which wasn't unusual in and of itself, most Czech women are. But… there was definitely something there. I was intrigued.

We sat down for coffee in the Star Café. She had big doe eyes and I was mesmerized as she told me about herself. Yulia was not Czech, as I had wrongly assumed, but Russian by birth. It just seemed natural to ask her to dinner that night, and we went out for Italian. She was twenty-five years old, of privileged upbringing, though she had lost her father when she was young. I could tell at once that she was fiercely independent and took pride in her education and autonomy. We went out five nights in a row. Five *dates,* in my mind. But at the end of the fifth night, she seemed to indicate coyly that the chemistry was not mutual, at least not in terms of a genuine future together. I was a bit crushed and did my utmost not to show the slightest sign of it. I found an excuse to go back to Seattle for a while and told her I would be leaving. We parted and I didn't think too much about her for some time.

When I returned to Prague, I was a bit cool. I let her know that I was back in the city, and where I was staying, but generally did my best to avoid her when possible. My pride was definitely getting the better of me. However, in my defense, she had also made it clear – there was no future between us. I continued on, spending money, drinking, going out. Generally living a debaucherous life and enjoying the freedom that that entailed. Thus, I was more than a little surprised when returning from a night out on the town to find her waiting in my hotel lobby. Fortunately, I was alone.

The next day, inspired by her show of affection, I bought her a beautiful dress which she returned immediately. Then, after a few days, symbolically casting the last of her reservations aside, she went back to the same store and bought the dress herself.

Six weeks later, we were married.

Hitting the Reset Button

There are very few things that light a fire under your ass the way the prospect of becoming a father does. It's probably evolutionary, or maybe it's biological. Whatever the explanation, not even the most intimidating drill sergeant in the world can make you hop-to faster than the mental image of your child going hungry. Though Yulia was not yet pregnant at the time we got married, we both agreed that kids would be a very real part of our future. Thus, although it was still hypothetical, the immense pressure I felt to provide for our children was very much grounded in reality. It was a sobering moment, getting married. It was time to get my life back on track; I stopped all the nonsense cold turkey and hit the grindstone like I was preparing for war.

The first order of business was clearing that ugly $100,000 in debt.

My dreams of becoming a professional golfer were firmly exiled to the land of "what might have been." I took stock of my professional situation and began to course correct for the future. Luckily, I wasn't starting from scratch. I already had the makings of a beautiful business idea, and since my three-year non-compete clause had officially run its course, I was free to return to my bread and butter: ocean freight invoicing.

Now, I'm with you. Nothing about that sentence has sex appeal. Ocean freight invoicing is exactly what it sounds like, it's about scouring hundreds and thousands of billing receipts, doing line-by-line analyses and finding minute discrepancies in the charges. It is not glamorous work per se, but it sure is lucrative as hell. After Yulia and I got serious, I said to myself, "I'm going to reverse this today." I was a man on a mission, and come hell or high water, I would wade through an ocean of receipts to do what I had to do for my family.

I started by calling in favors from old business contacts. "Hey Jim, can I do this project for you?" or " Mike, I've got a killer deal for you and I'll even reduce my fee." On and on it went. If I couldn't get anyone to bite, oftentimes I'd offer to do a smaller audit for free. Circumventing the system once again, I'd dial up a company's CEO directly and introduce myself, "Steve Ferreira, CEO of Ocean Audit, listen, did you know that one percent of your working capital is tied up in rogue freight charges? What if I told you I could get that money back to you in less than two weeks?" It was a bold move, and in that regard I was playing exactly to my strengths.

The thing is, there are only about five serious experts in ocean freight logistics in the world. I'm one of them. The industry is incredibly niche and as such, word gets around quickly. My reputation and proven track record were usually enough to get a foot in the door. If I were still met with apprehension, my value-added proposition was typically enough to sway their opinion. It was a win-win for the company, I reasoned. I offered my services for free, and if there was a refund to be paid out, it came from the vendor and not from the company's budget. If there was no refund to be found, then at worst I wasted five minutes of time, right?

After I got the green light from the powers that be, I'd maniacally go through the company books, detailing each and every erroneous charge that I located. Maybe I'd turn up $7,000 here and $4,000 there and another $1,000 towards the end. In total, I just found this company $12,000 in bogus charges, and I offered it to them as a gift, a small but not insignificant golden parachute. It was proof of concept, and it was a sure fire way to get my foot in the door. The company was ecstatic because they just got back $12,000 of free money they didn't even know they were owed. On my end, I knew that there was sometimes well over $100,000 more in refunds to come from those same invoices. I would hint at that and say, you know, now that I've proven what I can do, let me tell you there is plenty more to come in those piles of receipts. Would you like to consider taking me on to do a full-scale audit for you?

I had it locked down.

It really doesn't matter what industry you are in, people like free money and they like their problems solved neatly and without fuss. Fortunately, I was in the business of making money appear out of thin air, while crushing invoice errors like ants beneath a boot. Little by little, the side jobs began to add up and within a few months I had not only wiped out my debt, but was on track to have a fantastic closing quarter. Those long carefree days of hitting balls on every manicured lawn from here to Paris had given me, if nothing else, a tremendous amount of time to think. I had dissected and rebuilt my old business from the ground up more determined than ever to see it through. I was back, baby, and it felt better than ever!

For a time, Yulia and I split our lives between Boston and Prague. When it was all said and done, we remained in the Czech Republic for almost ten years. During that time I was able to successfully run and operate Ocean Audit as a solopreneur. I never had a single employee, an HR division, a board of directors, or any trainees. My overhead was extremely lean because the equipment was all inside my own head. Losing everything I had financially and being able to build it all back up (and beyond) within the short span of a few years gave me extreme confidence that I was doing exactly what I was meant to do. Golf was great, but at the end of the day I had put my 10,000 hours into becoming an expert in one thing, and it had nothing to do with sports. Things had definitely taken a turn for the weird those three years, but meeting Yulia was like coming up for a breath of fresh air. I suddenly knew all over again exactly where I wanted to go and how I was going to get there.

Putting It Into Practice

The entrepreneurial path is not one for the faint of heart. By definition, you're going to put in long hours, be forced to make incredible sacrifices, and the outcome of your success is anything but guaranteed. There are many factors that are beyond your control: the global market, world-wide pandemics, war, disease, famine…all these seemingly unrelated details can rally together to brew the perfect storm for your business. And you know what? Unpopular opinion here, but being an entrepreneur is lonely. Whether you're the CEO of an Amazon-like empire or a lone wolf like me, inevitably the pressure of victory and defeat rests squarely on your shoulders. As I said before, I don't have employees and as a result I've never had the burden of worrying about whether or not I would make payroll. But there have absolutely been times where I didn't know how I was going to pay the credit card bill or afford my children's tuition fees. It's an awesome responsibility to own a business and it's not a mantle that you should assume lightly.

All right, enough doom and gloom.

Here's the takeaway: when shit gets hard, the only lifeboat you will have will be the bedrock of whatever "why" brought you into that sphere of business in the first place. In other words, when you're battling the forces of chaos that threaten to capsize your business, the way through is by digging deep and leaning into your intrinsic motivations. Without these, an entrepreneur is no more sturdy than a straw man propped up with a broomstick. You've heard it before and I'm sure this won't be the last time it gets tossed around in conversation. Developing a solid personal "why" is paramount to your business's success. That thing, whether it's a person, an idea, a value, or a belief – that's what will keep you strong. The intensity of your "why" is what separates die-hard entrepreneurs, the successful CEOs and presidents, from part-time weekend warriors.

Those three years of vagabonding around the world, subsisting off the fresh air of fairway greens and pungent cocktails, blowing through hundreds of thousands of dollars…they were fantastic. I won't lie to you, I felt like a rockstar entertaining those women and teaching Microsoft executives the game of golf. But those years were also, in retrospect, devoid of deeper meaning. Like Odysseus's soldiers that were consumed by the lotus fruit, I lost my way for a time. It wouldn't have been hard to continue that extravagant lifestyle, seeking out pleasure and making just enough money for the next big trip, the next big score. And then I met Yulia, and we started our family, for which I thank God every day.

My family has become the enduring "why" factor of my business and personal life. Everything I do, I do for them. It's an electrifying responsibility, but also a humbling privilege to be able to provide for the ones I love most. They are the reason I get out of bed in the morning and the reason I stay up late at night working. They are my "why." That said, I don't think anyone else can give you the motivation to stand up in the face of adversity, of which you will doubtless encounter. No one, not even Mr. Motivation himself, Tony Robbins, can give purpose to your business if you haven't done the digging yourself. Maybe your "why" will be your family or a loved one. Maybe it will be the prospect of accomplishing a life goal, like buying a home or paying off your parent's mortgage. Whatever it is, your motivation is your own private responsibility; no one else can provide it for you.

Take it from someone who has learned the hard way: never underestimate the value and all-encompassing power of your "why." It can quite literally change the course of your life.

8 The Mental Jujitsu of Going Pro Bono

"If you're in the luckiest 1 percent of humanity, you owe it to the rest of humanity to think about the other 99 percent."

Warren Buffett

"No one is useless in this world who lightens the burdens of another."

Charles Dickens

****

Anyone that has paid even scant attention to life will understand what I mean when I say that our universe is governed by terrifically paradoxical laws. You cannot know light without understanding shadow, love without feeling pain, nor fullness without first feeling the aching of an empty belly. It is the same with giving. We've all heard the age old adage that he who gives without thought of return will receive in kind more than he lost. But here's the kicker. This is more than just a piece of the proverbial "manifest your own success" wisdom. It's an extremely powerful and often neglected principle of B2B relationships. The hard truth to swallow is that no one wants to work with an unproven talent. Maybe they will someday, but certainly not when you're just starting out. No business owner in their right mind wants to be the human petri dish on which you conduct your experimental trial by fire. This is often a major barrier to entry, not only for entrepreneurs that are just getting their feet on the ground, but even seasoned professionals who have exhausted the health of their relationships.

So how do you tackle this professional roadblock?

Nine times out of ten there is a creative solution to getting around the "No!" and we'll touch on that later. Sometimes, what's really required might seem downright contradictory to your overall game plan: you have to give something away for free. This is the mental jujitsu of going pro bono. What do you have to offer someone that currently has nothing, or no willingness, to offer you back in kind? What can you *give away* without damaging your company's health? Think about it this way. Let's imagine that you came across a fountain that instead of spewing water, churned out brilliant gold coins, ad infinitum. I bet that once you realized this fountain was bottomless in its wealth, you would come back again and again. You would bring your friends and family, the whole tribe would share in the riches of this one majestic discovery. Let's not overcomplicate the allegory: *be the fountain!*

If your mission as it pertains to your professional relationships is to always be the person that is offering help, solutions, wisdom, counsel, resources, etc., (e.g., the golden fountain), then people in your network (and even more importantly, in *their network*) will continue to flock to you. It might seem contrarian, but it's not. It all comes from giving with no thought of return or recompense.

How well and how much you give will determine what comes back to you.

Picasso Was No Engineer

My first impression of Judy was that I found it mildly ironic that her entire business was grounded in health and wellness. The woman looked for all the world like she could use a few weeks of sleep, a juice cleanse, and a mani-pedi. The bulk of her business came from the sale of patented vitamin supplements which she manufactured in Asia and had freight shipped to the United States. The only problem was Judy didn't know the first thing about container shipping and the dark circles under her eyes were evidence of the fact that this had been causing her some serious stress. Her business was doing well from a sales perspective, but she was hemorrhaging money transporting her product from Asia.

I was twenty-five at the time and had been settling into my role with Sea Land for about two years. Judy came to us looking to have her problem fixed; she wanted to stop the bleeding. When I reviewed her list of invoices, I was able to find a few minor fraudulent charges, but nothing that would really make a sizable impact in her margins. She wasn't paying inflated rates, and for the most part, wasn't being taken advantage of. Freight shipping can be costly, especially if you don't know the tricks of the trade.

Judy was grateful for the savings I was able to find for her, but it was obvious from her expression that she was immensely disheartened. Technically speaking, my job was done. I had evaluated her invoices, ensured the successful delivery of her product at the best available rates, and confirmed the pick-up and loading day. But…it was somewhat heartbreaking to watch this poor woman's dreams crumbling in front of me. Without really having any game plan whatsoever, I reviewed her file for an hour or two longer after she had left my office that day. I went through the invoices again and again without turning up anything new. "Shit," I thought to myself. "There's really nothing I can do for her."

I was about to give up and call it a day when something caught my eye. Scrolling through her files, I had accidentally clicked on a photo of Judy standing in front of her shipping container filled to the brim with boxes and boxes of vitamins. She was smiling back at the camera, clearly filled with pride at having made her dream a reality. But it wasn't Judy that caught my attention. What I noticed, first and foremost, was the container. More specifically, the empty space. Though the image was slightly pixelated, I toggled the mouse over the boxes and zoomed in. I could just make out what I estimated to be a solid foot and a half of empty space near the ceiling of the container. What the hell…why was there so much room in there? Why hadn't she packed more boxes into the container if she had that much space?

Boom! My eureka moment had arrived!

Judy had no idea how much money she was losing by not taking advantage of the full space within that container. She paid for every cubic inch inside that corrugated steel box. Thus, not jamming it full was the very near equivalent of cutting a hole in both of her pockets. I zoomed out of the image, rummaging around furiously in my desk drawer until I found pen and paper. I looked up at the image, then down at the paper, then up at the image again. Okay, yeah I can do this, I thought.

Well as it turns out, I'm not Picasso. My chicken scratch container would have taken last place in a stick figure drawing contest, and that was being generous. Although I personally could not draw it for her, I knew that the math, and more specifically the geometry, was there. I just needed someone else to translate my vision so that I could show Judy how she might maximize every inch of that space.

Sea Land had a staff of graphic designers and engineers capable of creating a perfectly workable rendering of my plan. The only issue was they billed thousands of dollars for each project, no matter how small, and that would be invoiced directly to Judy. Costing her more money was the exact opposite of what I was trying to do. Instead, I decided I would hire someone else. I quickly surfed the web's various freelancing platforms until I found a graphic designer willing to take on the project. He estimated the total at about $150 and said he could have it to me by the end of the following business day.

Two days had passed when I called Judy on the telephone and asked if she could come to the office that afternoon for a brief meeting. I told her that I had found something she might be interested in hearing. Judy showed up a few hours later and I presented her with a plain manila envelope and told her to look inside. She gave me a puzzled look but opened the envelope anyway, pulling out a beautifully stylized rendition of her shipping container filled to the absolute brim with product. I might not have been Picasso, and that artist was certainly no engineer, but damn did we do a good job together.

Of course, Judy had no idea what the hell she was looking at.

To her, it was just a picture of her vitamins in a shipping container. She didn't understand at the beginning. So I explained to her everything that had happened, going over the receipts again and again looking for errors, stumbling upon the photo and eventually hiring the graphic designer. Even more than that, I had taken it upon myself to crunch the numbers for her (thank you accounting degree!). Based on my calculations, by simply adjusting the way that each shipping container was packed and loaded, we would be able to fit about thirty-three percent more product into each container, effectively skyrocketing Judy's profit margin per load.

It was worth every penny of that $150 to watch her eyes light up like that.

And that wasn't all. Judy was so impressed and taken aback by my work ethic and willingness to help her, even beyond the duties of my station, that she made it a personal point to go and commend me in front of some of the highest executives in our office. The result? I was given a promotion and moved to a managerial role in a larger office in downtown Boston. That meager $150 out of my own pocket money had been paid back threefold with interest.

That was my first introduction to the substantial power of giving in the development and cultivation of B2B relationships.

So You Want to Be on TV?

What are your thoughts on public speaking? Does the prospect terrify or invigorate you? Most people probably fall into the latter category, but for me, speaking in public has always been a source of great joy. It's something that I honed debating through four years of college, and it's continued to be a healthy medium for me to express myself creatively. Regardless of how you feel about the prospect of "performing" for an audience, most people can't relate to or identify with the desire to give back once you've reached a certain metric of success. The business world, however, is abound with these gracious types of individuals, the mentors that take young potentials under their wings and guide them through the sometimes perilous waters of entrepreneurialism. Be it free consulting services, a one-to-one mentorship, or offering your wisdom at regional conventions, the idea of giving back to the community to which you belong is not a revolutionary concept. But it is a tactically effective one.

I like people. I also like talking. For me, the prospect of public speaking, particularly if it means I can help other people in doing so, is extremely enticing. I often get paid a speaking fee if I'm invited to a conference or a seminar, especially if it's a large or high profile event. But even when I'm not paid, I'm still every bit as eager to get my hands on that microphone. I've been practicing the habit of public speaking for many years now.

Before the global blitzkrieg that is COVID-19 rocked our world, I was a frequent visitor of the New York Public Library. No, I didn't go there for the fiction, the musty smell of old literature, or even the pursuit of higher knowledge. I was there to speak – about business, about B2B relationships, about actualizing that entrepreneurial dream. The New York Public Library, like many other community-run organizations, has taken it upon themselves in the last decade to offer a myriad of weekly professional development seminars, courses, and free lectures. The library frequently hosts a diverse spread of successful business professionals who come to offer their expertise to the public – you guessed it – *free of charge*. And it's not just the major metropolitan hubs of the world who offer this type of free expertise. Even the local library in Hartford, Connecticut (where I live), has similar weekly events.

Given the choice between a TED talk with thousands of high-profile professionals, or my local library, it's a no brainer. I'm doing the TED talk every time. However, I am also a very strong believer in the idea that you are never too good, too knowledgeable, or too successful to give back to other people, most especially to those that do not have the professional acumen that you do. Think about it this way. I would rather practice my presentation on fifty groups of local entrepreneurs then to take to a major stage and have it be the first time I've spoken to a live audience in my life. The point I'm making is that helping others very often leads to helping yourself, directly or indirectly.

Here's an example.

Recently, I was giving a presentation at a local seminar. The library budget was so pitifully low that

I didn't even dare to ask for a speaking fee. It was good practice, I figured, and I had the opportunity to help some people who hadn't learned some of the more difficult business lessons that I had had to. So, I took to the stage and I gave my presentation about entrepreneurialism and the common pitfalls of B2B relationships. All in all, I was satisfied with my performance and felt that the people in attendance appeared genuinely pleased. They had gotten something meaningful out of it, I hoped. After it was over, I stayed on the stage a few minutes longer to answer some follow-up questions from the crowd.

After a few minutes of back and forth, I saw a tiny, fragile-looking hand raised somewhere in the back of the audience. The wrinkled hand belonged to an elderly woman with wispy white hair and a pastel sweater. She lobbed her shaky voice up at me from her chair in the back of the room, "Mr. Ferreira," she began. "I just have one question for you. I was wondering if you could tell me how to start a business." She was dead serious.

Well, they say there is no such thing as a stupid question, and generally I am of the belief that that is true. No one should be made fun of for trying to learn. Still, this was a meeting for entrepreneurs who had already started a business, not a Business 101 class. I heard more than a few snickers from the crowd and saw several grown men roll their eyes in indignation. The question seemed innocent enough on the surface, but explaining to someone how to start a business was like opening a rabbit hole that you might not come out of for several days. The reaction of the people in the crowd pissed me off, though. Didn't all of us, at some point or another, have to answer that very same question for ourselves? Wouldn't it have been helpful for someone to just tell us in a succinct, comprehensive way, how to accomplish the task?

I was determined to answer her question with respect.

I took a moment to collect my thoughts and then answered the old woman with a ten-minute, step-by-step approach on how she could legally start her own business. At the end of my answer, the room erupted into applause. Apparently, what had been deemed a stupid question, was actually quite a great deal more valuable than people were willing to give credit to. I had done my best to take an extremely complicated question and boil it down to its simplest, most digestible form. I wasn't getting paid for any of this; it was pro bono "work" that I thoroughly enjoyed doing. Thus, I had no expectations that anything would come from that meeting.

Fate had other plans.

Among the local NYC denizens in attendance that night was one of FreightWaves TV's top reporters. After the presentation, he came to speak with me directly and congratulated me on my speaking ability. "I was really impressed with the way you handled that last question," he said. "You did a really wonderful job of taking something complicated and confusing and making it accessible to everyone." Not one to turn down free compliments, I told him thank you and that I appreciated his coming out to attend the seminar. Nice guy, I was thinking to myself. Before I could pack up my things and go, however, he shoved a business card into my hand.

"You ever thought about being on TV?" he asked.

And just like that, I found myself the host of a television show, *Navigate B2B*, on the increasingly popular FreightWaves TV, a network dedicated to the data-driven analysis of global business trends. Once again, by doing something without any thought of personal return, I was reaping the benefits of pro bono work. I had gone in with no intentions other than offering personal advice to the community and practicing my speaking skills. In total, it cost me about $40 in gas money. The results, on the other hand, have been too vast to quantify.

Give. Give. Give. Give back to your community.

It's Raining One Euro Coins

Build it and they will come. Build it by being a content/industry/tv expert and they will come twice as fast. That's my motto anyway.

When I took to the stage in Amsterdam, it was to speak at a freight shipping industry event. I wasn't particularly worried or nervous about the speech. In

The Mental Jujitsu of Going Pro Bono

many ways it was routine, sort of standard run-of-the-mill content. I had taken the gig as an opportunity to gain more exposure and to offer my knowledge to anyone who might benefit from hearing it. Though this audience was well versed in the ins and outs of ocean freight shipping, I was still firmly situated in the top five percent of industry experts and knew that I had a few things to offer that they had never heard or seen before.

I had agreed to do this event without requesting a speaking fee, and had even paid my own airfare to get to and from the conference in Amsterdam. The investment for this speaking opportunity was significantly more expensive than the $40 in gas money it had taken me to get to the New York Public Library. That being said, the audience were vetted industry professionals and I also knew that this "free" event could potentially be a major driver in revenue if I played my cards right. After all, there's no law against being philanthropic *and* profitable, right? I certainly didn't think so.

I decided to supercharge my speech, not by any hilarious antics on stage per se, but with a strategic little marketing maneuver. Hours before the event was to take place, I had taped one euro coin to the bottom of each and every chair in the conference room, along with a short message. By the end of my presentation I was feeling a bit meh, however. My speech had fallen on somewhat deaf ears and I didn't have the feeling I had captured the attention of the audience in the way I was striving for. As the organizer of the event stepped on stage to take the microphone and introduce the next keynote speaker, I motioned that I just needed a minute more.

I looked out over the sea of European faces, taking a long moment to make eye contact with several members of the audience. I picked up the microphone once more and in a subtle whisper, I asked, "How many of you here today believe in the idea of free money?" Chuckles from around the room. I even heard someone say, somewhat sarcastically, "Of course the American is talking about 'free money.'" I pressed on. "Really, show of hands here, how many of you guys believe in the concept of free money?" Only a few hands went up in the audience. "Hmm… a lot of skeptics in our industry, I see." The crowd laughed. "Ok," I began, "I challenge all of you, the believers and the skeptics, to look underneath your chair right now. Go ahead, do it, and tell me what you find."

One by one the audience reluctantly folded themselves underneath their chairs and searched for….what? They did not know. There was a low rumbling and then a quiet roar that grew louder and louder as everyone found their one euro gold coins. Lots of smiles and shaking heads. Everyone turned their attention back to me. The note, which had been attached to each of those gold coins, read, "This may only be one euro, but contact me for the other 49,999 you're owed."

Needless to say it created quite a buzz.

That one free speaking event, combined with a little provocative marketing, generated well over six figures in Ocean Audit revenue for me. Before you ask for anything in a professional relationship, first evaluate this one question: what value can you give someone else first?

Putting It Into Practice

My entire business is built around the concept of offering something before I get my own reward. From day one, my company policy has been that I do not charge for any audit unless I find an actionable refund. That means if they don't get paid, neither do I. From a business perspective, that's a powerful statement to make. It sets the expectation from the very beginning that my clients and I are working on the same team to reach the same end goal. I am not trying to scam, overbill, or collect more than I'm owed. I'm out there to find money they didn't even realize had been swiped from their pockets.

At a fundamental level, the mental jujitsu of going pro bono is twofold. First, it is about protecting your would-be clients from the sharks. Unfortunately, the B2B environment is littered with unsavory, predatory characters that are out to take advantage of unsuspecting business owners. They will do whatever they have to do, morals be damned, to get the transaction done and their commissions paid. Particularly in my industry, this means that there are an incredible amount of blind spots and pain points where a company can fall prey to extortion and fraudulent charges. I'll fix that, and I'll do it for free – at least at the start.

One of the surefire ways that I attract new clients is by offering free value up front. If a shot caller within the company is willing to allow me to go over their books, I will give them a refund owed by one of their vendors, amounting to a couple thousand dollars. No questions asked. If they decide afterwards that they don't want to use my services, that is their prerogative. Fortunately, that almost never happens. More often I'm met with, "Ok, but what's in it for you?" The same thing – money! That little chunk of change I just found my future client is nothing when compared to the huge refunds I know are just waiting to be plucked from their invoices. And when I'm hired, I keep fifty percent of what I find.

Professional B2B sales people *solve*, and it's that domain level expertise that keeps you front of mind.

The second tenet of going pro bono is the exposure. Whether you're flying internationally to European trade conferences or giving an entrepreneurial pep talk at your local high school, the most important component is that you are out there, in the spotlight, available for people to find. It's not any new age wisdom about manifesting your destiny, or speaking your dreams into reality. It's cold, hard statistics: the more people that see you as an expert, the greater the likelihood one of them will become your client. It's a numbers game, and it can be played on a very lean budget.

I'll end this section by saying I don't approach my pro bono work with the expectation that someone will owe me something afterwards. That is not a gift, it's a bill. I have been blessed to have a healthy number of professional relationships that have started from doing something for someone that was going to give me nothing in return. And that's how it should be. Pro bono means doing it for free. You can't fake that mentality; people will see right through you.

The paradox, then, is that the moment you stop trying so hard is the moment where it falls naturally into place. Give and open up the possibility of receiving in return.

9 "No" Is Just a Yes That Needs More Convincing

"It's hard to beat a person who never gives up."

Babe Ruth

****

I don't really believe in the idea of a "no". When a prospective client hits me with that most irksome two-letter combination, I let it roll right off my back. To me, "no" just means, "Steve, you didn't do a good enough job convincing me to say yes." When someone says no, rather than get angry or frustrated, I simply take ownership of the situation and think to myself, "Hey, I haven't done a very good job here. I need to step up my communication." The reason I choose to look at rejection this way is because I genuinely believe in the product I'm pushing. Ocean Audit is about helping people get money back that has been wrongfully taken from them – at no charge to their business! If I can't convince someone of the value in that idea, then my communication has not been properly tailored to the respective audience, or I'm talking to the wrong person.

Which leads me to my next point.

In large organizations it's remarkable how the reactions or judgements of one set of "decision makers" can differ so wildly, and often contrarily, from another. Thus, an integral part of my business model is scooting around the inconsequential "nos". What I've learned from experience is that there are usually a myriad of roadblocks between you and the person you need to speak to, the person that has the authority and responsibility to sign your contract, to pay your invoice, to form that partnership. In my industry, this roadblock often takes the form of a logistics team. While they do not have the power to say "yes" in bringing my auditing services on board, they certainly like to flex their power to tell me "no". It happens all the time. They don't want some outside consultant coming in and poking holes in their work, pointing out where their own inattentiveness might very well have cost the company thousands of dollars.

Tough shit.

Challenge Everything

Challenge *everything*. Nothing is set in stone until it's been written into a legal contract and signed by the appropriate parties. Until that time, your one and only goal in subverting the "no" is to position yourself as close to the person who ultimately has the power to make that deal. Unfortunately, I've had to learn this the hard way. On more than one occasion I've found myself pitching to a room full of twelve or more board members. Perhaps eleven of them are in agreement that this is a worthwhile proposition, but there's always that one pain in the butt person that has to say no. On more than one occasion, a single negative vote cost me a deal that was worth six figures in potential refunds. I learned very quickly in my career that anytime you have more than two people in a room, you go for the light touch, no serious pitching, absolutely no selling. Getting one person to say yes can be difficult enough, imagine trying to convince five, ten, even twenty people! It's like setting out to shoot yourself in the foot.

When someone consistently tells me no, I figure I have two options: I can tailor my approach and really make it personal to the individual…or I can go over their head and find the real decision maker.

The Man Who Hated Sea Land

Steve McLaughlin hated Sea Land the way most people hate mosquitoes.

In his estimation, the sales force of my (then) proprietor was the human personification of walking turds, and as such he wanted nothing to do with me or our business. Unfortunately for Sea Land, Steve was the CEO of a large coffee trading company. He was also the president of the California Coffee Association. This essentially guaranteed that if there was a coffee import coming in anywhere from Seattle to San Diego, Steve would know about it. Not only that, he was in direct control of all the vendors in use.

I never figured out just who it was that had so royally pissed him off, but at twenty-four I was assigned to his account and given the directive to go out there and get Steve's business back no matter what the cost. I explicitly remember, I was told not to take no for an answer.

The first time I showed up at his office building, Steve sniffed me out like a bloodhound. "You're from Sea Land, aren't you?" he said, skewering me with his eyes. The man was like a psychic, reading the contents of my soul before I'd even shook his hand. I didn't even get the chance to respond to his question in the affirmative before he was telling me to get lost. "Oh, I hate you guys, get the hell out of here!" By all accounts, it was not a very successful first meeting, and yet… I had seen something in his eyes. It was a look that seemed to be searching for a reason to trust me, to relate to me. Deep down, I could sense that he didn't hate *me* personally, he was just put off by whatever pompousness Sea Land had waved in front of his face in the past. It was a small chink, a crack in an otherwise intimidating and fiery personality. But it was something.

The next time I showed up, I brought doughnuts. Again, the moment my foot touched the polished floor Steve was on me like a hawk, "Ah, what the hell are you doing here again?" I raised the box of doughnuts in a decidedly non-threatening gesture. "I didn't come to sell, Steve. I came to learn the nuances of coffee. What can you tell me about these beans from

Costa Rica versus the ones over there from Panama?" He eyed me with thinly veiled skepticism. "What are you talking about?" he practically growled. I was no dummy, though. I had it from a reliable source that every Friday Steve would host a coffee tasting in his office, to which he would invite various customers to come and sample the product. He was like a coffee guru and I made it a point to be there every single Friday. Always with doughnuts.

At first he refused to let me join the tasting. "It's not for you, it's for the customers," he'd bark at me. But I knew better; this was a game of willpower, who could hold out longer? Over time, I began wedging my way into his office with less and less resistance. Around the sixth or seventh appearance, he finally cracked. "All right, you've been here enough times now… I guess you can sample a few of the brews." I'll never forget those tastings. He'd have a selection of ten to twelve glasses, poured out in these beautiful little demitasse cups. I'd mosey up to him after I set the box of doughnuts down in plain view for all to see and say, "Hey Steve, what are we trying today? Kenya? Jamaica? Blue Mountain?" I was a smooth-talking, twenty-something, but my experience with coffee was limited to the confines of a Styrofoam cup.

As it turns out, there's an art, an etiquette even, to coffee tasting of which I was completely ignorant before I met Steve. I was surprised to find that you're not even supposed to swallow the coffee, you just taste briefly and spit it out! Well, I let him teach me all about it. I could tell the guy was passionate about those beans, and I wanted him to see I wasn't just another sales putz from this big corporation. I don't think he really knew what to make of me, but he liked the free doughnuts and besides, what harm was I really doing?

As I slowly became more and more comfortable around him, I'd lob in the occasional shipping reference: "Man, this Kenya brew is so bitter, but that Jamaican Blue Mountain? Whew, can we ship that for you? Might even have to divert a little bit of it to my house." It was light teasing and he was a good sport about it. The weeks turned into months, and I began to take him out regularly for dinner and drinks, sometimes with his wife and whatever girl I might be seeing at the time. This guy was the ultimate big cheese and back then I was just a young, scrappy kid. But I think he respected the audacity, my tenacious persistence. I wasn't going to give up. I was determined to make him see that Sea Land was *me*, not whatever crummy experience he had had previously. If he was going to do business with Sea Land, he'd deal with me directly. In truth, he already hated the company so much that really the only place to go from there was up.

I worked that "no" for over two years. By the time I left California and moved to Boston, Steve had given Sea Land so much business via coffee shipments that it was almost more than we were capable of handling. But I stuck to my word, I made it a point to ensure that Steve only dealt with the A-team of the business. I introduced him to the VP of Operations and said, "Listen, I don't know too much about coffee. But these guys do, they are experts. They will ensure your product gets handled with the greatest possible care." I didn't try to be an expert in something I was not, instead I just got out of the way and put the right people together.

In a lot of ways, Steve epitomized the idea of "challenge everything". It was obvious from the first time I met him that his gripe was not really with our services, or even with me personally, but rather was a result of poor communication. No one from Sea Land had taken the initiative or the time to properly apologize and earn the man's trust. When it comes to circumventing the no, as with anything good in business, it's going to take time. However, if you already know that you're speaking with the correct shot caller, the one with the right authority to make the decision, it's always worth the effort.

A no is just a yes that needs more convincing.

Whose Chain of Command? Not Mine

Several years ago I landed a major deal with a Fortune 100 chemical company, Dow Chemical, a company with a workforce 100,000 employees strong. I was brought on to do an audit of some of their expense reports and it turned out to be incredibly fruitful; I found over seven figures in actionable refunds. While this was a major milestone in my career, it almost didn't materialize because I was talking to the wrong people.

I had approached Dow Chemical the same way I approach many of my clients, via tailored, personalized messages in the form of email video content or directly on LinkedIn.

Unsurprisingly, my first barrier to entry was a logistics team. They worked me around for a few days before expressing their regret that Dow Chemical was not currently in the market for an audit, even if there were refunds to be found. They would handle it internally, I was told. Well, that sounded an awful lot like a no to me, and the worst kind of "no" at that. I wasn't being rejected because my business was not useful to the company, I was being turned down because someone's ego was getting in the way. I recognized immediately that this person was not the shot caller, they had no real authority to hire me even if they had been in agreement with my proposition. So, I went right over their heads, about three levels to be exact, until I reached the CFO directly.

You could make the argument that my business was not exactly an urgent matter that required the attention of a CFO who managed a multimillion dollar company. Sure, you could make that argument… but I would do it again in a heartbeat. Unlike his logistics team, the CFO recognized the value proposition right away and we were able to sign a deal within a week. Soon after, the refunds began flooding in, and both Dow Chemical and myself were reaping a very significant profit from those invoices. Not long after, however, things started to get weird. The CFO had appointed a team to supervise my work and prepare weekly progress reports for him concerning the continuing audit. As we neared the final segment of invoices, I started receiving cryptic messages from this appointed supervisory logistics team. "After we get this last refund and pay you, we are going to end our agreement with you," they'd say. "We are already doing similar services internally and with other vendors. We don't need your expertise."

Talk about mixed signals.

For weeks I heard the same rhetoric over and over: we're going to void your contract, we don't need you, we can handle this ourselves, etc., etc. There was a part of me that wanted to be equally petty, to return their childish behavior with my own and just say, "Oh yeah? Let's ask your CFO what he thinks about that." But I didn't. Instead, I just waited and waited for the termination letter that never came. As recently as this year, one of the members of that logistics team reached out to reconnect with me on LinkedIn. He was retired now, he told me. "Steve," he said on a phone call, "I didn't mean to be so hard on you back then, you know? It's just that we didn't really like the way you had gotten the deal done, you understand? You really did go above all of our heads. But I won't lie, I always liked you and you did great work for our company." You've got to be kidding me, I was thinking to myself. You mean to say that all of your antics were nothing more than smoke and mirrors because of a bruised ego? Rather than anger, his random admission left me with a feeling of incredulity. If anything, it just confirmed my original belief: he was not the shot caller.

It might seem like a risky strategy, circumventing the chain of command like that; there are times that I would most assuredly agree with you. If I was a small business for example (in terms of revenue), or just starting out, you can be sure that I wouldn't be lobbing my emails to the top Fortune 100 companies' C-suite executives. It would be inappropriate and unprofessional. Now, that doesn't mean I wouldn't find some other creative solution to bypass their initial reluctance (hello again pro bono), but I am not a new business. I've established myself as an expert in my field, I have a very solid presence on LinkedIn, and I am the host of a television show dedicated to navigating B2B relationships. If it's not too cocky to say, I've earned the right to sit at the table and at least be heard.

You're Ghosting Me

"Fucking logistics people, unbelievable."

I sat there staring at my computer in semi disbelief. I'd just been stood up – no, even worse than that, I'd been altogether ghosted. I had set up a Zoom meeting with a logistics manager for a major pet supplier. The meeting had been planned several weeks out and I spent a good deal of time doing the preliminary research, figuring out how best to tailor my pitch. When the appointed hour arrived, there was no one there. Nothing but digital crickets. I reached out to the logistics guy, asking if he needed to reschedule. I received nothing back in the way of a reply. The way I saw it, one of two things had happened: he or a family member had suddenly contracted COVID-19 and he wasn't able to make the meeting or…. he simply didn't want to be shown up, as might be the case if I was able to find a few hundred thousand dollars in refunds.

My money was on the latter.

Luckily, I had already contacted this company's C-level team who had put my service in motion – I just had to finish off the effort. Thus, I felt it entirely reasonable to reach out to him directly and explain the situation over LinkedIn. I didn't bash his logistics manager or try and get in a cheap shot, I just told him that the meeting had been cancelled without explanation and that I was very disappointed because the numbers led me to believe there were some seriously appetizing refunds to be collected for his company. What happened next was amazing. The C-leader was extremely gracious and told me not to worry about the issue; he would look into it for me. In less than half a day, he had overridden that logistics manager's decision and I was able to move forward in structuring a great deal.

Ironically, it turns out I had actually met this logistics manager in person when he worked for another client. Perhaps he was a bit embarrassed that six-figure refunds were identified at his previous company as well.

I remembered the man. In terms of personality, we were like oil and water. We never had a formal dispute, but I remember that neither of us took a particularly strong liking to the other. Suddenly, it made a great deal more sense why he might have declined to show up for our scheduled Zoom call. I don't care what anyone says, ego plays a massive hand in your professional relationships. Whether it's yours, the CEOs, or someone who's nineteen rungs below him - it matters. That's why I don't believe in accepting a "no" at face value. If you have a product or a service that will undisputedly solve a problem for your would-be client at little or no cost to them, and you're still getting served nos, I think it's a safe bet to assume you've stepped on someone's toes.

Part of becoming a good sales person, and more generally a business professional at large, is understanding when and how to subvert a negative response. Sometimes, the situation calls for you to buckle down and make that relationship flower, even if it's going to take you two years (as was the case with Steve, the coffee guy). Other times you need to be able to discern if your no is simply coming from the wrong mouth. If that's the case, how can you creatively sidestep and get your message to the right people, to the place where it's going to be most effectively received?

Putting It Into Practice

Getting around the sometimes arbitrary sometimes inexplicable nos that your potential clients refute you with can be exasperating. Trying to make someone see the logic of your plan can feel like teaching an old basset hound how to use a flushable toilet. People are people, and that invariably means that they are going to be stubborn and risk averse. Your job then is twofold: convince them that the idea was theirs all along (oh yes, stroke that ego) and be clear in how you are going to actively address their pain points. I have a deceptively simple strategy to accomplish both: research. The extent of the research you do, prior to ever sending that first introductory email, text message, phone call, or LinkedIn request, will determine your overall success. Here is my four step approach to getting around the no, or better yet, never having to hear it in the first place:

- Identify the pain point.
- Find the shot caller.
- Tailor your pitch.
- Shoot your shot.

1. **Identify the pain point.**

    My industry is very specific. On the surface, it is about transporting goods from one part of the world to another for an agreed upon price and at an agreed upon delivery date. Yet, if you asked any executive in freight shipping what their biggest headache is in the industry, I would be willing to wager that billing would rank in the top five every single time. I know this because I spent years collecting bogus charges for my clients and fighting on their behalf to get back the funds they were owed. It's a major headache and not something that any CFO wants to deal with if they can help it. That is my industry's pain point. That is what I am here to solve. When I pitch to my client, I prediagnose the problem like a doctor or a surgeon would and tell them exactly how my business will fix it. Before you approach any new customer or client, you need to be absolutely certain that this is a pain point they actually feel. Maybe others in your industry have that same problem, but perhaps not this client. It's imperative, then, that you do your research. It doesn't matter how slick of a talker you are, if you are offering to fix a problem that doesn't exist, you're going to get nothing but a big, fat bowl of nos.

2. **Find the shot caller.**

Once you've identified the specific problem of the organization you're trying to make contact with, it's time to dig into their personnel. Finding the right person to be the conduit for your message is arguably as important as the message itself.

Selecting the wrong person can sometimes mean the difference between scoring a major deal and declaring bankruptcy – it's that important. That said, the shot caller is not always the person at the executive level. In my industry, targeting the CFOs makes the most sense as my product is directly related to financials and fraudulent invoicing. If you're a marketing agency, however, in most cases it doesn't make much sense to be reaching out to the CFO, the COO, or even the CEO. They have designated professionals for that. Before you even think about tapping that send button, thoroughly vet the company's organizational structure and determine who is the key player in your decision.

3. **Tailor your pitch.**

Time to get personal. Once you've located the right person to carry your message where it needs to go, it's time to craft the perfect pitch. Now, on this subject different experts have different opinions and I can only tell you what has worked for me: being highly personal. Before I decide to reach out to my person, I will scour their LinkedIn, Instagram, Facebook, *Forbes* articles… anything I can find with information about them or their family (I promise, it's not really as creepy as it sounds). The end goal here is not a little light stalking for kicks. The goal is to find a piece of descriptive detail that makes the whole thing personal. Do they have kids that like to play hockey? Do they have a wife that is a marathon runner? Maybe a son or daughter who goes to the same university as your kids? The minute you start weaving personal details into your pitches, it automatically sets you in a class above the rest. It shows how much you care about this meeting and how much research you've done to prepare, especially on somebody you've never met before. Forget what you've heard, business is nothing if not personal.

4. **Shoot your shot.**

Like a Viking warrior going into battle, you must pick the "weapon" that will be most effective in combination with your personal style. I have found, for me personally, that LinkedIn in conjunction with highly personalized video email messages are the sweet spot. LinkedIn works because I have amassed a huge following on that platform and am considered a thought leader in my space. Thus, if I reach out directly from LinkedIn and someone decides to peruse my profile, they find a whole ledger of evidence that I am who I say I am. The engagement, total followers, and stream of freshly uploaded content speak for themselves. In that way, I am setting myself up to "shoot my shot" with the greatest chance of success. Likewise, I have found email to be equally effective when used in tandem with video messages. I've mentioned it before, I'm a talker; I like people. I also happen to think I'm pretty good at speaking to them, so the video messages are great for that. Sure, it might take me a bit more time to edit a video and record a whole presentation, but I will tell you that seventy-five percent of the people that open my cold emails become clients. Seventy-five percent! That's no accident, it's preparation. I tailor not only the message, but all of the smaller details, even down to the time it should be sent, to maximize my overall chances of a positive reaction. Shoot your shot, but before you do, determine the medium and platform that will most effectively translate your personal brand.

There it is. That's my patented formula for circumventing those pesky gatekeepers. Now, go out and try it for yourself!

10 "Oh Shit! We're on the Air?"

"The only thing you can do is take a learning experience from it, positives and negatives, and apply them to the future. What did you do right, what did you do wrong, and I did a lot of things right this week."

Tiger Woods

****

Tiger Woods has always been a hero of mine. Contrary to what you might think, it's not just a fanboy golf crush. To me, Tiger has always been the living, breathing embodiment of unobstructed concentration and power of will. Of course I admire his skills in playing the game, but even more so, I admire his killer instincts, his champion mindset. Speaking of mindset, I heard an interesting story about Tiger's childhood and his training regime while growing up. According to legend, Earl Woods, Tiger's dad, was adamant about instilling in his son a laser-like focus when he was out on the course. In order to accomplish this, Earl would instigate any number of tricks, distractions, and antics while Tiger was preparing for his backswing. Earl, it seems, had a particular fondness for lobbing objects of various sizes at Tiger's back when he wasn't paying attention: coke cans, car keys, tennis balls, you name it. If that didn't work, he would bust out his handy dandy air horn and really scare the bejeezus out of his son. This went on for years.

The result was that by the time Tiger had reached the professional level, he had trained so furiously, in such an unorthodox manner, that nothing short of a meteorite falling from the sky could distract him when he was about to take his shot. He had mastered the art of supreme concentration, the single-minded focus of a champion, and the results would speak for themselves for the next two and half decades.

Swing and a Miss!

I couldn't sleep the night before.

Call it a premonition of what was to come or just late night indigestion, but whatever the reason, two melatonin did nothing to take the edge off that night. Sleep remained annoyingly aloof. I had done the preparation, checked and rechecked my equipment, by all accounts I was prepared for tomorrow's TV broadcast. It was to be the latest episode in my show, *Navigate B2B,* and I had arranged for a leading industry expert to join me on the air. My guest had made her millions in the supply chain and logistics field. The plan was to discuss the inherent similarities and differences of navigating professional relationships in our respective industries.

When the morning of the big day finally arrived, I pulled my sleep deprived carcass out of bed and into the warm embrace of a steaming cup of coffee. Stepping into my office, I surveyed my virtual studio set up. The camera stood mounted to the top of a tripod underneath the soft glow of an umbrella reflector. My notes, positioned at eye level behind the camera, were printed in large oblique fonts so that I could quickly glance at them should I need a transition or a quick talking point. Behind me, a large abstract painting and a small unassuming lamp provided a cozy and intimate quality to the recording. My microphone was old school, a square metal frame with a neatly threaded steel ball in the middle, like something out of an old disc jockey set up. I took a deep breath, fifteen minutes until we were live.

Typically, the guest is sound checked the day prior and comes on a quarter of an hour before the live show. I imagined how she might be feeling this morning. Was she nervous or excited? Had she ever spoken on live TV before? I had prepared with her all week and set up her technical training with the producers of the show, but on the whole, she didn't seem overly comfortable with the controls she was responsible for. I mentally sent a prayer to the big man upstairs that everything would go off without a hitch. Five minutes now until we're on. I'm in sound check myself, the audio engineers and producers speaking in my earpiece, "Mic check. Check? Steve, can you hear me okay? Alright, we're getting a good reading. We're good to go."

The final countdown: three, two, one…

"Good day to everyone out there listening, my name is Steve Ferreira and I'm the host of *Navigate B2B*. It's such an honor to be here with you today…"

As soon as I'm on the air, the nervousness melts away like butter softening in the sun. I'm channeling my inner Tiger Woods, all concentration, all focus. This is what I love to do, helping people navigate their professional relationships both in and out of the global trade and logistics industries. This is my domain, this is where I am an expert. Everything is going perfectly. We roll through the opening segment, and I'm mentally reviewing the questions I'm going to cover with today's guest. One last final check, multitasking while I smile and speak to the camera. Right in the middle of my segment, I hear a voice carried through my earpiece. It's the producer.

"She's not ready. Steve, the guest isn't ready yet. We're going to need you to stall."

Oh shit. There's that feeling again, where your stomach suddenly seems to lurch down several stories in the blink of an eye. I don't miss a beat, though. I just keep on rolling. I'm talking about Amazon stock and some of the strategic marketing techniques that they employ to keep people engaged. I stay there for a moment, talking about the holidays and the efficiency of the company in keeping their deliveries so consistent during the pandemic. I make a joke about the mountain of boxes that came to my house. Christmas presents for my kids. I laugh in a good-natured way. I'm stretching this thing thin. Surely, she's got to be ready by now?

"Steve, this isn't going to cut it. She can't get the tech to work…"

This is turning into a major clusterfuck and fast. The producer is in my ear constantly now, making it hard to think. "I don't think she's going to be able to do it. The tech isn't working, she isn't…it's not happening." Outwardly, I'm smiling at the camera and doing my utmost to remain poised and in control. I have to project authority, I have to maintain my equilibrium. In all my nightmares, I have never imagined myself left dumbstruck or empty handed on live television. I'm mentally kicking myself; I had a feeling this was going to happen. Though we spent four or five days going over the questions and reviewing the video set up, suddenly nothing was working. It was do or die… time to call it quits or…

"We're going to have to cut it, this isn't going to work…"

Not a chance. As I approached the segment and talking points that I was supposed to cover with my guest, I decided to take a leap of faith. "There really are only two experts on the planet that could answer this next question, and I'm one of them. Let me jump in and answer it, while our guest gets situated." I took the bull by the horns, kicked it into overdrive and bulldozed through the next thirty or so minutes, alone. It was some of the snappiest quick thinking I'd ever done in my life. When we finally cut to black and were officially off the air, I could hear the producer clapping in the background. "Well done, Steve! Well done!" I let out a huge sigh of relief. I was both overjoyed and exhausted.

As it turns out, my guest had simply panicked. It didn't matter that we had done countless video tests, mic checks, question preps, and the whole nine yards. When it came time to do the big show, unfortunately, she was mentally scrambled. Now, she and I are not strangers. I've known her for years and she is quite a savvy professional, one of the best in the world at what she does. However, while she's an expert in her field, I'd venture that she doesn't do much in the way of *public* speaking. It's a whole different ball game when you've got a live audience on the other end of that screen, and the pressure sometimes gets to people. I could certainly remember how intimidating it had been my first time on air and I sympathized with her. Without some seriously quick thinking, it could have been an embarrassing disaster not only for the network, but for both of us professionally.

When I look back on my life, I see a myriad of different experiences: moving to a new country (several times), speaking in public, taking risky appointments with mafia members, auditioning for a strip club, wining and dining some of the biggest and best in my industry. When I add all of that up, the victories and my fair share of defeats, what I see is a lifetime that has trained me to be *comfortable being uncomfortable.* I didn't have an Earl Woods figure scaring me half to death with an air horn, but what I did have was a whole heck of a lot of hands-on experience. Panic, and it's reciprocal – focus – is something that you can train and learn to control. I talked about the power of improvisation before, and I think this story firmed up my belief in just how necessary it is to cultivate that mental resilience. It doesn't matter what industry you belong to, the power to think quickly on your feet, project authority, and take command of the situation is going to steer you in the right direction one hundred percent of the time.

Train yourself to respond well under pressure and nothing can defeat you.

Leveraging Crisis - Why COVID-19 Is the Best Time

Speaking of pressure and unforeseen circumstances, it's time to address the big, ugly elephant in the room – COVID-19. Unfortunately, 2020 will be defined in the history books by a global onslaught that took the form of a seemingly innocuous virus. This virus, small as it might be under a microscope, threatened to bring the global economy to its knees. Of equal or even greater import, it has also cost the lives of hundreds of thousands of people around the world. Thus, I do not mean to make light of or try to undermine the tragedies that have taken place. On the contrary, I fully acknowledge that for many people, 2020 might have been the worst year of their lives from an economic, health, safety and personal standpoint. But where there is crisis, there is always opportunity for those who are savvy enough to look for it.

A recent article by Greg Miller, published on FreightWaves.com, suggests that despite initial uncertainty, certain sectors of the economy are more primed than ever to make a historic comeback.

"No one predicted a U.S. import surge in the middle of a pandemic — but it's happening. The big question now is: How long can this last? The answer has key implications for ocean spot freight rates and contract renewals, port throughput, and landside volumes for trucking and rail.

Investment bank Jefferies issued an exceptionally bullish report on Wednesday implying that import flows should remain heavy all the way into 2021. Inventory restocking isn't about to peter out. It's just getting started, according to Jefferies.

'We are just at the beginning of what is likely to be one of the biggest restocking cycles — if not the biggest inventory restocking cycle — in U.S. history,' maintained Jefferies Chief Economist Aneta Markowska on a conference call held Thursday to discuss the report."

In other words, for those prepared to do so, 2021 might just be the opportune time to launch your business. Why? Simply put, the global economy is going through a transition, a rebirth of sorts. There is an aggressive demand for goods and services that have been out of reach, or available only in limited quantities for over a year. Particularly for the shipping industry, the supply and demand of goods being brought into and out of the country is primed for a huge rebound. In fact, global big hitters like Deutsche Bank have gone on record saying that they believe the resupply of American inventory levels will put the shipping industry on a "containergeddon" type path – which is fantastic news for anyone in a contingency business.

As I sat down to write this book about my life and all the lessons I've learned from its peculiar twists and turns, I couldn't shake a particular feeling, an overwhelming desire to give back. I have been very fortunate to be able to provide a good life not only for myself, but for my family as well. As a solopreneur, I've done this entirely on my own. I never had a boss, an HR department, or a board of directors. It was always just me. However, in the back of mind lives a nagging question…Could you repeat your success? Could you teach it to someone else? And if so, how would you accomplish that?

Like many people around the world, COVID-19 forced me to take stock of my life and the things that are important to me. During this period of self-reflection, I realized that as an industry leader, as an entrepreneur, and as a recent TV personality, I have the opportunity at hand to give back to other aspiring leaders. I not only have the means, but the platform to share my success and my knowledge. As a result, I've decided to open Ocean Audit for franchising opportunities. My goal is to help other entrepreneurs create the financial freedom and wherewithal to become their own success story. Drawing on my 30+ years in the industry, and an army of freelancers, I've been able to put together a robust model so that anyone, regardless of whether you have zero experience in ocean freight shipping, can step into the framework and replicate what I've done. I'm not saying it will be easy, it never was for me, but the contingency business is a sure thing. It's guaranteed to pay dividends.

Consider this. If Markowska's prediction is correct, then 2021 will witness a huge rise in the number of globally shipped containers. That means a mountain of invoices and a huge opportunity for human error or intentional overbilling. It's simple math; the more containers being shipped the more likely it is that one of them is due for a very satisfying refund. And it's not just ocean freight. either. Business supplies, consumables, transport – all of these are contingency-related businesses with massive potential in the coming year. My franchise is just one opportunity of many that you can take advantage of. It doesn't have to be me, but I cannot encourage you enough to get out there and (responsibly, of course) go after those entrepreneurial dreams. Despite the prevalent media narrative, the business world is primed for a counter punch.

Don't let it pass you by.

Putting It Into Practice

Not everyone wants to start their own contingency business, or work in ocean freight invoicing for that matter – I understand that completely. It's an industry decidedly lacking in sex appeal. However, for those individuals who still feel a burning desire to go out and actualize their dream of becoming a self-made man/woman, there are plenty of other avenues. Rather than trying to brainstorm for you, or reinvent the master blueprint of success, I'll just tell you plainly and honestly what worked for me (if you've made it this far, I'll assume you care what I have to say). Here are the five final takeaways I wish I had known:

- Have a master plan.
- Develop a media presence – it's free!
- Alone doesn't really mean "alone".
- Test it on someone else's dime.
- Solve, don't sell.

1. **Have a master plan.**

    I can feel the eyes rolling already! It's so true, though. Time and time again, I see entrepreneurs jump neck deep into the water before they've even learned how to swim. The probability of your success can be directly traced back to how much time you spent developing your business model and execution plan. Remember, before I left Sea Land, I spent over two years developing exactly how I was going to get the thing (Ocean Audit) off the ground. I worked my day job full time, and then came home to burn the midnight oil, doing calculations and metrics projections. A master plan is everything, and I do mean *everything*! At this stage in your business (or your would-be business) you have the luxury you will not have later – time. Use it wisely. Check and recheck your numbers. Test your hypotheses on a small scale if you can. Lay out your budget and determine how much working capital you need to amass before you go looking for a loan, then double that amount. And absolutely, without fail, have someone that you trust vet your business model. Whether it's a mentor, a successful family member, or a hired consultant – get that extra pair of eyes!

2. **Develop a media presence – it's free!**

COVID-19 threw a massive wrench into my B2B in-person appointments. I had previously relied on my natural gift of gab to carry me from one referral to the next. Suddenly, like the rest of the world, I was forced to make drastic changes at the onset of the pandemic. Enter, *the power of LinkedIn*. I'm not at all shy about it, LinkedIn is far and away my favorite media stepchild. It's an incredible professional resource, and an accessible tool for anyone that has a few hours and an internet connection. I've talked about this before, but some of my most profitable engagements and deals have come directly from comments and posts about my LinkedIn content. Becoming a television host has only furthered that discussion! As a business owner, the media is your friend. Yes, my preference is LinkedIn, but depending on your industry, maybe yours could be Instagram or Twitter, heck even Tik Tok. The point, however, is that developing a media presence, while time consuming, does not cost you a single dime if you do it yourself. Moreover, it's an incredible tool to position yourself as an expert in your field to an essentially captive audience. Media allows you to test out ideas and theories in the form of "op-ed" type pieces while getting instant feedback from your target audience. It's a powerful resource, and business owners that neglect that truth are doing themselves a major disservice.

3. **Alone doesn't really mean "alone".**

Contrary to our culturally popular lone wolf stories, nobody in business makes it on their own, not even me. While I have been a solopreneur from day one, that by no means implies that I've somehow gotten this far without help. In fact, over the course of my career I have probably hired and fired an entire army of freelancers. Finding good people is tough, and if your budget is strapped down tight (as it will be when you first start out) I can't recommend enough the benefit of using one-off workers. From graphic design, to website development and content writing, there are a myriad of online platforms where you can hire cheap, talented workers to build out the weightier parts of your brand. Personally, I've found this to be an invaluable resource in locating virtual assistants who help me keep track of the twenty million things I have on any given to-do list. Just because you're stepping under the mantle of entrepreneurialism does not mean you have to wear every single hat in your company. In fact, that's a sure fire way to burn yourself out, and reduce your overall efficiency. Use freelancers! That's what they are for. Yes, you will have to wade through some crappy ones to find real talent, but the same is true of any situation in which you are hiring new employees. The difference is you don't have to provide freelancers with benefits, which translates to lower overhead for your business. Going it alone does not really mean going it "alone". Use the resources at your disposal.

4. **Test it on someone else's dime.**

I've talked about this previously, but it's worth reiterating once more. If you can find a means to test your system or theory in such a way that you are not losing money in doing so, then by all means do it! When I started Ocean Audit, I was fortunate enough that the company director saw value in the idea and let me test the business model within the larger framework of a Fortune 500 company. This is the exception, not the rule. However, with a little bit of creativity you can find a means to test your concept on the micro level before you apply it to the macro. Think of this like the COVID-19 or influenza vaccination – no medical body in the world is simply going to allow someone to propagate a new medicine before it has been extensively tested. In much the same vein, it's borderline irresponsible for a business owner to found a company on a product or service that has never been genuinely market tested. Thus, it's my firm opinion that before you worry about the name or logo of your exciting new LLC, first test it's efficacy in the real marketplace – preferably on a small scale, and with someone else's money (willingly given, of course).

5. **Solve, don't sell.**

The best businesses in the world don't sell anything, *they fix problems.* Too often I see business professionals drinking their own Kool-Aid, absolutely convinced that their revolutionary product is going to creatively disrupt the entire industry. These are the same individuals who are flabbergasted when the product falls flat on its face. If I could give just one piece of advice, it's to understand that before you have any business idea, you should first have a problem. Almost like when reverse engineering a computer, you need to understand what piece of the hardware isn't working, and why, before you can start proposing solutions. A good product should never feel like selling, it should feel like offering obvious value. Using Ocean Audit as an example, I was absolutely certain that there was consistent overbilling taking place in the industry. Thus, when I finally founded my company, I didn't have to pitch hard to my prospective clients. I simply told them the truth: someone took your money and I'll get it back for you. There were, and remain to this day, skeptics and critics. When they saw the $140,000 I found in refunds in just under ten minutes… well, that always does a good job of shutting them up. Solve a problem, don't sell. And if they don't believe you, have something you can offer for free. Give them a taste, a small proof of concept, and then reel them in for the big ticket item.

****

So that's everything! My life story in a nutshell. As I said in the beginning, the journey was never meant to be a linear line to success, and I don't think that model is realistic for most of us anyway. Life is more akin to a meandering river than a tunnel forged through the heart of a mountain. In the same way, my story has taken me in a myriad of directions which I honestly never could have predicted.

I didn't follow a presupposed path or subscribe to the popular narrative of how I should live my life. I charted my own course, and learned as I lived through each experience. There were some victories and certainly I had my share of mistakes as well, some more colorful than others. As such, I hope that in reading this account of my story you've been entertained, but even more so, I hope that you found it useful in application to your own career. Remember, no one in history has ever made a name for themselves by coloring inside the lines, by playing it safe one hundred percent of the time.

Don't be afraid to go out there and bend the rules a little bit. Challenge everything! You might just be surprised by what you find outside the lines.

Who Is Steve Ferreira?

Steve Ferreira is the man you go to when there's money to be made. In the two decades since the onset of his solopreneur career, Steve has recouped over $50M in lost revenue for his clients by pinpointing some of the largest undetected errors in ocean freight shipping. His thirty-six years in the industry have made him a global logistics guru, positioning him as one of the most highly sought-after ocean freight analysts in the world.

His unique approach to ocean freight invoicing has garnered worldwide attention and put him in the media spotlight with CNBC, *Forbes*, and *USA Today*. Perhaps even more impressive, Steve's company, Ocean Audit, has assisted seventeen of the world's Fortune 100 Companies including the likes of Nike, General Motors, and Dow Chemical. Today, Steve can be seen hosting FreightWaves TV's *Navigate B2B*, a nationally televised show that helps others develop their own B2B business personas. Steve coaches entrepreneurs worldwide, as he remains dedicated to changing lives, one client at a time.